Unraveled

A Journey Led By Faith and Hope

SYLVIA R. MERINO

ISBN: Paperback: 979-8-89079-125-2
ISBN: Ebook: 979-8-89079-126-9

The author's memoir is about her life and work incidents that left marks in her heart, mind, and soul. Some incidents stem from her childhood all the way through the last 60+ years. Some characters and locations have been changed. Some of the events and places may not be 100% accurate and are products of her present recollections. Also, her family circumstances and emotions may differ from her siblings, family, and extended family.

Table of Contents

Part Two

Preface

After 48 years of working and looking back at my personal life, I was inspired to write this memoir. I felt inspired to write about that child and how she came to become a successful woman in her own terms and giving thanks to those who helped her through her journey.

Why did I put so much effort in every job I had? Then it came to me, that because I found myself lost in a family of eight, and the 2nd child of the three girls and later the three boys joining us, I felt lonely and unheard. I felt like I had to compete with my siblings, but I rarely won.

I grew up feeling like the ugliest person on earth, and I was not very smart. I struggled with math and reading (comprehension). Going to special classes in high school made it worse thinking the bright students were laughing behind my back. I couldn't finish college because Rheumatoid Arthritis knocked at my door, and it forced its way into my body. I couldn't hold a pencil to write until months later when the medicine took effect. By then, I was already comfortable in all that I was doing, working two jobs and dancing with the Pima Community College Bailet Folkorico. As you can see, I made myself very busy. It kept me from home issues.

Dad was initially very moody and a lot of it was when he drank and the guilt for not having more to give us. His life turned around years after I had moved out of the house. Mom was and always will be opinionated without thinking it's hurting the receiver. Many times, that is me, although, I also hear it from my sisters. The boys had it all. Mom treats them like kings. They can do no wrong. Am I jealous? Sometimes, but most of the time, we joke about it.

Throughout my working life, I focused on the job, the people I worked for and my peers. This kept me from thinking of home and people who hurt me. At work, people didn't know my life before my working years. They never asked nor did I share unless that person was my best friend. I didn't think they cared or that it was important for them to know.

Both Mom and Dad had their spiritual sides. They had good intentions. They wanted the best for us. Throughout the years, we learned lessons taught to us without words. It was through our parents' actions that I learned what I know today. I had to teach myself other important aspects in life. I had to learn to be affectionate, for one. I had to learn to love myself as God made me. Mom instilled in me that I should never think I was good at anything because there will always be somebody better. So, I (we) rarely received praises for our accomplishments. My praises came from work. Affection came from my peers and managers and later from my dates and friends. Eventually, we taught our parents to hug.

When I was old enough to stay in Mexico with my grandparents, I stayed for days during my summer school breaks. Mexico was my escape. I had freedom but not without consequences. After my high school senior year, I stopped going as often unless it was for a funeral or Mom had an urge to visit with her family.

While writing my story, I found myself thanking all those who I worked with. I've always had a deep love for people, sometimes even for those who did not like me. For those who didn't like me,

I felt sorry for them that they had so much hate for themselves that it extended to me and others. I prayed for them.

Because I couldn't finish college, I spent many years comparing myself to my siblings who earned a college degree. Then I was fortunate to have one college manager who worked to find me a position at a large corporation. Once I passed through the corporate doors, I faced challenges that I accepted with determination, passion, and discipline. My faith and hope kept me going from small challenges to the biggest challenges that I never dreamed of and each time succeeding. There were a few bumps in my journey, but I always found a way to work through them.

We can all start somewhere, just look beyond, and work your way up. Some think their jobs are boring and quit and start all over and keep stepping back instead of moving forward. To keep me from that cycle, I played games by challenging myself when work became mundane. It was so pleasing when my game resulted in a refined procedure or eliminating unnecessary tasks, resulting in new projects, new challenges, and renewed passion.

Most importantly, I have unraveled the ugly thoughts of myself. The proof is in my writing and my soul can now sing praises for all my accomplishments that could only happen because of my faith in God and my passion.

PART ONE

Some grow up know_ng their destination, walking the path a little too quickly only to find that some adventures were missed. Others go with baby ste⊃s, perhaps too slow and at the end discover they missed it all. Some go questioning the path for most of their lives; at the end some are surprisingly satisfied and others disappointed.

"Who am I?" I am not a known celebrity nor an important figure in society nor am I a counselor or a medical advisor writing a self-help book. I am a simple person, a stranger sharing the story of finding myself through a journey. It is my story that could be told differently from my siblings' point of view.

It began by my hiding behind a mask, hiding how I was branded by family, friends, and later by strangers and the unfortunate circumstances that kept me from reaching a college degree. Not having it meant I had to work twice as hard. "What will I become?"

While finding the answers, I went through insecurities, humiliations, and challenges. The challenges became knowledge that resulted in self-discoveries and then I learned passion. Passion to free myself from the past and the passion that I put into every challenge I was faced with, especially when I was telling myself I couldn't do it.

Being the second of six children, I sometimes felt left out because of the attention given to my older sister and younger sister. It was our parent's adult friends who triggered the initial thoughts by their actions that caused the feelings of being less than my siblings, especially when school grades and education were discussed. I was also the target of name calling, causing hurt and resentment and later being bullied.

Am I more than the clumsy, naïve, gullible and the black sheep of the family? Did I allow them to make me who I am, or did I become what I saw in the mirror? How did the immense grace of love given to me by my Creator help me overcome barriers?

As a child we believe what we are told. We grow up believing that the surroundings we live in are all there are. Then there's the one day when you find yourself at a friend's home and you see a different world. Some better, some worse.

Not having affectionate parents, I grew up longing for it. Later as I entered the world, I slowly learned what affection felt like. It was through my managers, both female and male, and instructors, then with the friends I picked up along the way. It also helped to have a spiritual family and friends.

Later in life I understood that some of the name-calling I experienced was not intended to be malicious but terms of endearment, mainly from family members. The remaining hurtful names and actions were from rude people with insecurities or those needing to be in control, or those who undermined me for their own advancement, or simply because they, too, were targets at one time and were now targeting others as if that were okay.

People can change. I witnessed my dad change, while I lived changing others, not knowing that I also was being transformed.

It was through grade school that I began my experiences in Rayón, Mom's hometown, and later in the workplace where I began to slowly unravel my wounded soul, creating the person I became.

Sylvia - June 1956

**Sylvia (1ˢᵗ on left) with Ana (3ʳᵈ to the right) and friends
and one of many Charlie Brown Christmas trees.**

SYLVIA (aka Silvia)

I was born on June 20, 1956, in Tucson, AZ. My birth certificate shows my birth name in white ink as "Silvia," barely visible between the white wrinkles of the paper's black background. I find my paper-thin birth certificate in dad's desk. There is also a picture of my older sister standing next to me in a small living room. There is only one couch, an end table and what appears to be a coffee table that a Charlie Brown Christmas tree sits on. I am chubby, my hair is light. I am leaning on my sister. We look happy and content. We lived off Main Street, on Simpson Street. There is a row of attached homes, maybe townhomes. We lived between two of them. Most pictures are outside where we spent most of our time. When I was about 3 years old, we moved to a red brick house on Lincoln Street on the Southwest side of town. It had 3 bedrooms and 1.5 bathrooms. Later, as our family grew, a bedroom was added. This is where I grew up and stayed until I married and moved to San Diego.

I was called many names, but it was one of my parents' older friends, Amparo, who visited us often who got the biggest kick in calling me "Chivita." I detested it.

"I am not a goat!" I'd say, and it seemed like she did it more just to aggravate me.

I also have full lips and a big mouth. I grew up getting teased, causing hurt and paranoia. Once I was told I was born with a plate under my bottom lip. I was told I looked like a horse when I smiled. This was from a family friend who said he would become a dentist and I would be his first patient but instead he became a teacher. Then it was the guy who would whisper to another guy, "there comes luscious," referring to my lips. Today, people pay to have lips like mine.

As if this weren't enough, Mom advised me in Spanish,

"Si sonríes te verás más bonita!" "If you smile, you'll look much prettier!"

I would lock myself in the bathroom to look at myself in the mirror. At that time, I was very naïve and believed that maybe I was the ugliest person on earth!

My skin is light. I was born with light red hair; it was very thick and unruly. Mom brushed my hair, always trying to put it into a pig tail, but the hair would shoot straight up. At times, she gave up and instead put on that darn barrette that felt like it was going through my scalp. I didn't dare scream, or I'd get that painful little pinch on my arm. Because I was lighter than my older sister, Dad used to tease that I was the milkman's daughter.

In later years, when I was invited to birthday parties or for special events, Mom had us walk to one of the neighbors for our haircuts. Gabriel, who then became Renae (trans), cut our hair. She did a great job! When we found out Gabriel had become Renae, Mom told us, pointing her finger in our faces,

"No anden criticando." "Don't you go criticizing." So, we never said a word, and that was that. We never thought much of the change, either! We liked getting our hair done by her. She worked miracles on mine.

I was a bed wetter, causing Mom extra work while pregnant with the next baby.

I was also the one with scabs on my legs from falls and I also had black knees. Mom thought my older sister was too dark. Mexican women don't like their daughters getting tanned, mainly the ugly dark tan that left us "roñosas," or dirty. Mom would point out my black knees in front of Ana, thinking Ana didn't like her darker skin and so she made it a point to compare my black knees to her even-colored skin. In retrospect, she was insulting Ana too because Ana liked the color of her skin.

"Mira que feas las piernas de Sylvia, y las rodillas tan roño-sas." "Look how ugly Sylvia's legs are with scars and her knees look so dirty."

The most humiliating time was when I stayed with my cousins. We played in the riverbed. Our skin turned darker as the sandcastles and tunnels grew and sand stuck to our bodies. Once inside, my nina (my Godmother), put us all in the bathtub. As

5

she washed the sand from our bodies, she said to me, "You are the cause for the dirty water." In my mind I was thinking that we all played in the same sand. She scrubbed and scrubbed my knees, and nothing changed.

"We all knelt on the same sand," I insisted. I was embarrassed and maybe a little humiliated.

I was also the first one to need prescription glasses. Around the 3rd grade, I began suffering serious headaches. My mom finally realized there must be something seriously wrong when I chose to stay home from school. I hated to skip school even when I was sick. I was taken to the doctor and that's when they discovered I needed glasses. When it was time to go to school, I worried about the name calling! Sure enough, the minute I walked into the classroom, someone hollered, "Four-eyed monster!" and the rest of the boys around him started to join in but were quickly stopped by the nun.

I was also a very angry child. Maybe because I kept all the negative name-calling and feelings locked up or because sometimes, I didn't feel heard. There were so many of us and with Dad working and Mom trying to handle chores and caring for infants, she didn't have time to listen to any of us. The attention I got from Mom was when she'd ask me to do something for her and I resented it.

I never and will never stop loving my siblings. It was mostly with my older sister that I compared myself to because we were closer in age. In our older years, she has in many ways repeatedly reminded me of my accomplishments and points out tasks and systems I dance around that she cannot master, yet she has a doctorate. I have learned a lot about life from her.

When we were teenagers and first started reading books, she secretly read an "adult" book that involved some romance and bandits. She hid it when needing a break. One day, I found it, and she caught me reading it. After that day, we have shared many books.

I was and still am the gullible one. Delbert, one of my brothers-in-law, always played pranks on me when we had our landline phones. For example, I would dial Laurie's phone number and a voice (Delbert) at the other end that I didn't recognize answered with the name of a brewery. I apologized for dialing the wrong number and redialed. This goes on until the 3rd try when I finally hear my sister, Laurie, laughing in the background. Today, Delbert and others find other ways to get to me.

Because of the name calling and feeling inadequate, I always felt like the black sheep, always avoiding attention. I never raised my hand in class. When I spoke, sometimes the English word got lost, but I was thinking the word in Spanish. Today, I use the excuse that I'm old, or have long haul COVID symptoms.

I also avoided being asked out on dates. What if they accidently touched my hair and they withdraw because instead of silky hair, it feels like a dried weed? And what about my lips?! Would they even want to kiss me? I did smile, though, because that made me prettier!

I met my husband, Ralph (aka Chito), who graduated from Arizona State University (ASU) with a Welding Engineering degree. We had one child. Adding to our family are mothers and fathers-in-law including Ralph's two siblings. Al, my brother-in-law, has two sons and two grandchildren and Bea, my sister-in-law, has two daughters and one grandchild. Al tells me I'm his favorite sister-in-law. That's because I am the only one, he has. They make for a lot of love, fun, and laughter when we are together.

Sylvia to the left and Ana – 1960

July 2023

ANA (aka Anna)

My oldest sister, Ana, was born in October of 1954. She was born with nice, tan skin, big dark brown eyes, and beautiful black wavy hair! When I was born, she tried to pick me up from the couch and dropped me. Fortunately, nothing happened to me, or maybe it did. Most baby pictures show her protecting me, always playing right next to me.

She spent most of her time reading and learning, while the rest of us engaged in daily chores. We tried to make her feel guilty, but she didn't care. She was content in her own little world. When she started driving, she ran all the errands since Mom didn't drive and Dad was at work. Dad drove her in the evenings and weekends.

She also had her embarrassing moments. Mom needed eggs from the milkman who had just dropped off the milk. She had Ana run out to buy the eggs. By that time the milkman was a few houses away. Once she paid for the eggs, the milkman had her get into the van and he drove her home. She hates when we tell this story because she was so embarrassed and worse because of the teasing she got from her family.

Ana did very well in school, although she did have it hard since we all grew up speaking Spanish to Mom and then repeating the same thing to Dad in English. When she went into her first year of school, she was caught speaking Spanish on the playground and was reprimanded.

We had a family friend, Anselmo, who visited us often. After the greetings, he'd ask, "How are you doing in school?" and if it was after a report card, he'd ask about grades. Of course, Ana was the one doing the best. He pulled out a dollar bill and handed it to her and for the rest of us it was the little change that came out of his pocket. My reports were low grades with "for your efforts."

I looked up to Ana, being the big sister. She introduced me to music that our neighbor shared with her and later bought her own albums.

When we were younger, we played doctor. During one of the sessions, Ana stuffed Kleenex in one of my nostrils. Mom thought I had a stuffy nose and got concerned that I was getting sick. After I told her that Ana put a Kleenex up my nose, she got a scolding but nothing that would stop her from making me do dumb things.

When I was about 7 or 8, I had a rash on my upper inner thigh from my shorts rubbing against my skin.

"Put Vicks on it! It will heal right away!" Naively and obediently, I did. Shortly after, I'm hollering, "It burns, it burns!" I complained, holding onto my crotch. Mom wanted to scold Ana but instead she began laughing. This is one story that comes up often.

One time Ana and I had an argument after dinner, while washing dishes. I got mad and poked her neck with a fork. I argued it wasn't a stab because there was no blood, and there were no fork marks, so I guess that was supposed to make it okay.

Then there was another argument that I knew I was right about something, and she argued I was wrong and at the end I told her, "When we die, Jesus will tell you who was right." I left it at that.

Ana went on to the University of Arizona where she received her bachelor's degree in early childhood & elementary education in 1976, then her master's and then her doctorate by 2004. For the first part of her work life, she taught elementary school and later taught teachers.

She married Phil, and they adopted two boys and have four grandchildren. She's currently a family-support specialist that includes developing and teaching trauma-informed parenting classes at her work site and is involved with out-of-state conferences. She has used her experiences in raising adopted children with new parents either adopting or who are now parenting their grandchildren.

Sylvia (1st left), Ana (top right), Laurie (left bottom) and Richard.

Laurie (left) and Sylvia – June 2018.

LAURIE (aka Laura)

Laurie is the 3rd daughter. She was born in May 1960. Laurie was born with her skin much lighter than mine. I was more of a yellow color. She was chubby and very cute. I don't know if we became pals because we are both Geminis, and it could be that Ana was in school for two years before I started. That left Laurie and me at home to play together until the first boy was born two years later.

We also did chores together when we were old enough to do them without supervision. She washed and hung clothes on the line. Washing was not just putting clothes in the washer and sitting down to read a book. To wring the clothes, they had to be put through a wringer. She hung the wet clothes on the clothesline, in our backyard. She helped Mom in the kitchen, while I swept the house. Later I helped her fold the clothes and ironed what needed ironing. I still enjoy ironing. I find it therapeutic.

Laurie was a cry baby. When I turned five, I was gifted a baby doll, the only gift I received. Laurie wanted it and so she cried when I didn't give it to her. Dad took it out of my hand and handed it to her. Oh, that hurt but I didn't cry, and I carried that hurt for a long time during my childhood. It wasn't that the doll was taken away but more because they didn't care about how I felt. After all, it was my birthday. My parents didn't care or notice. Later, when I told this story in one of our family gatherings, Laurie took note so the next year for Christmas, she gifted me with a similar doll. I still have it.

She cries watching certain movies, but Wizard of Oz? She still doesn't like to watch it; she knows we'll tease her when she cries.

Laurie is also the sports enthusiast of the three girls. She watches sports with her family; she'll even go online to make bets and proudly tells us when she wins small cash. When her boys played football, I liked going to watch them. I don't know the plays, so one day, the nephew not playing sat next to me and gave me plays for basketball. I believed him until everyone on our bleacher started to snicker and laugh when I realized they were pulling my leg.

There are two incidents that I think about with Laurie. The first was when she was in the 4th or 5th grade, she needed to go to the dentist. Since Dad worked and Mom didn't drive, we walked. She must have had 4 teeth extracted in preparation for braces. As we walked home, she walked ahead of me, sobbing. It was sad watching her walk with her head down holding onto her cheeks. She looked so cute in her green uniform and white tennis shoes with white bobby socks. When we walked into the house, Mom was nervously waiting. She knew it must have hurt and Mom hurt more because Laurie had to walk home in pain. It was one of the few times Mom let it be known that she felt sorry for us.

The second incident was when Laurie asked me to cut her bangs. When done, she saw they were crooked, so she threw the scissors at me. Thank goodness they didn't land on me, but it sure did scare me when they came flying at me. She gets embarrassed when I tell the story. She also liked taking our clothes. We knew she had worn a sweater when we found Kleenex in the pockets. She always had a runny nose, which we later found out was due to allergies.

As kids we had fights and arguments, but I don't recall any of us holding grudges longer than a day, usually for just a few minutes.

Laurie married her high school love, Delbert. She was forever in trouble at home because she took over the phone after school and then again in the evenings. The phone was in one room, and she slept in the room across the hall. The phone cord was stretched long enough to pull it in under the covers while she secretly talked to her boyfriend. Dad would get furious, but she paid him no mind.

When they got married, and drove off to go on their honeymoon, I cried as if they were leaving forever. They had four children. Two boys and two girls. Now they have four grandchildren.

Laurie graduated from the University of Arizona, with a bachelor's degree in business and a master's in technology.

RICHARD (aka Ricardo)

Two years later, in June of 1962, Richard was born. Our parents were going crazy especially Dad, having his first son. I remember he and my tía (aunt) dressed the three girls in red dresses Mom had made us for Easter. Dad took us to the hospital to visit our new brother. That is one of the times that I remember seeing him so happy.

When Jerry and Richard did something bad that Richard initiated, Jerry always got blamed. I stepped in and told Mom or Dad what really happened, and they still walked away without reprimanding Richard, the instigator.

One time Richard didn't want to share a basketball with Jerry, so he ripped it with scissors, so neither one of them could play with it.

He was also very curious. One day he stuck his hand in the washing machine wringer, and it took his whole arm and only stopped because the wringer couldn't turn any further. Dad was furious. He learned never to do that again.

Richard went on to the University of Arizona and became a Mechanical Engineer. He met his wife, Cathy, and got married and had eight children. They have seven grandchildren.

Jerry (left) and Richard caught playing with mom's flour.

JERRY (aka Gerard, Gerardo)

Mom had a Holy incident in 1963. She was painting walls in the house while eight months pregnant and began to bleed, so was rushed to the hospital. She saw a statue of St. Gerard (known as The Mother's Saint). She said a prayer to help her safely deliver, and Gerard (Jerry) was born on November 12, 1963.

Jerry, like me, was a 2nd child and the one I protected from Richard, defending him from being the troublemaker when Richard was the cause.

Jerry graduated from Pima Community College and went on to work at the Tucson Jail as a prison guard. He retired very young and continued to work. He currently transports illegal immigrants to wherever their destination may be. It could be to a holding facility or to an airport to transport them back to where they came from.

Jerry met his wife Deborah (aka Debbie). They had four children and now have six grandchildren.

STEPHEN (aka Steve, Steven, Esteban)

The last child, Stephen, was born September of 1970. He was brought home the same day I began high school.

Since he came seven years after Jerry, it was welcoming to have a new baby around the house. He was the modern child. He came when Dad was making more money and was less grouchy. A week later Mom had to go in for a hysterectomy. Stephen was left in our care as an infant. We all took turns feeding and dressing him, but Laurie was the one holding him the most.

There are pictures of Stephen dressed in mismatched clothes. We wonder why he or we didn't dress him more coordinated. I say we used to buy some of his clothes at Yellow Front, but Mom says she bought them at Sears or Penney's. I think of Yellow Front as today's Dollar Store. It could be that we were given money to buy him birthday gifts and so we went to Yellow Front because it was cheaper. In one picture Stephen is wearing a checkered shirt and striped pants, riding a tricycle. I feel sorry for him when I look at this picture. Mom made all the girls' clothes but never for the boys. When I began working, I bought him clothes that matched, sticking to solid colors.

The boys were very disorganized. When I folded their clothes, I liked emptying out their drawers and neatly putting everything back in. When they married, their wives hated me because my brothers expected neat drawers with neatly folded clothes, but the wives were too smart to give in to a routine that the husbands could do for themselves.

Stephen was born with small eyes. Richard thought he looked Asian so one day he told him he had floated in from China in a wicker basket and that's where Mom and Dad had found him. Stephen was very young, so he was puzzled and went to ask Mom. "Quien te dijo eso?" "Who told you that?" Mom asked. Mom told him Richard was just kidding with him.

I think a DNA test is needed because I and some of our family members have also been asked if we are part Asian. One of our uncles had an ancestry book made for the Roche side of the family, our family's last name. The book showed our initial last name was Rochester then changed to Roche. So, who knows what the mix is and so that will be my next project!

Stephen loved to play with the small Hot Wheel cars. He carried a few in his pants pockets. When at school, he took them out to play while the teacher taught and got caught more than once.

One year when he was in the eighth grade, the nun told my parents he wasn't going to amount to anything when he grew up. That angered my parents, but they were respectable and kept quiet. When Stephen graduated from the University of Arizona with a Mechanical Engineering degree, my parents were so happy, and I bet they wished they could wave his certificate in the nun's face! Plus, Stephen was called shortly after graduating to temporarily substitute in a math class at this same school and probably for the same nun.

Mom thought he would become the family priest but soon after, he also met his lady Giselda (aka Gui) and married and had two children. No grandchildren yet!

There is more on my brothers' lives but because they were so much younger than I, it will have to be their story to tell.

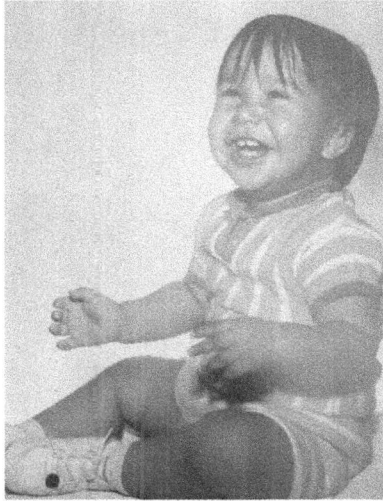

Stephen 1975

First family picture with the 6 children – 1975.

Last family picture before dad's passing. Looks like I just said
something funny…Maybe just the face I'm making! – 2003.

Our Parents

"*A good father is a source of inspiration and self-restraint. A good mother is the root of kindness & humiliation.*"
—*Dr. T. P. Chia*

Father

What I write about our Dad is what we learned when he was in his '70s. Some we discovered after he passed away. Dad never discussed his past with us. I think if he had shared his upbringings and the struggles he went through, it would have helped him mentally. Whatever thoughts and feelings he harbored resulted in outbursts directed at family, mainly Mom. His discussions began with his sons-in-law and later with one of Ana's adopted sons.

While writing Dad's story, I think about families who come from wealthy or even middle-class families. The children are so far ahead. I remember Betty, a friend of mine from my Atlanta travels who shared pictures of her family. Her dad was dressed in a suit and her mom in a pretty skirt and matching jacket. Possibly a pretty necklace around her neck. Betty, standing between them in a pretty dress, was about 10 years old. These children have already learned business terms, society terms and I can only imagine the level of their vocabulary. I don't know anything about her parents, it was just an observation from the pictures I saw. At 10 years old, my picture looks quite different.

Sometimes I wonder how our lives would have turned out having everything a child wished for. I am also sure that these families had their share of struggles, trying to live up to their lifestyle, personality issues, and maybe addictions and family issues, regardless of status.

It took for Betty to show me her family pictures to realize how different our worlds were as children, yet, at the end, as adults, we were equal except I'm the minority. Our upbringing was quite different but it's not all materialistic things or clothes we wore or whether her dad was a blue or white-collar worker, it is more about the values and morals that were taught.

Dad - late '40's

21

And here is my Dad's story, bringing me back to "who am I," knowing so little of our Dad. He was not starving or homeless, but he was abused by those who cared for him and experienced so little of being loved and appreciated and had no one to encourage him until possibly his last foster parent. My passion comes from Dad's passion to succeed for his family and at the end for himself.

Our Dad is Ernest Roche, born on November 7, 1927, in Tucson, AZ. His grandfather came from Ireland, jumped a boat and stayed in Guaymas, Mexico. His father, James (my grandfather) married Serafina who lived in Mexicali, Baja California, Mexico.

James and Serafina moved to Phoenix and worked at the Southern Pacific Railroad, then transferred to Tucson. They stayed with an aunt, but she became abusive with Dad's mother, who was suffering from ovarian cancer. Serafina washed Southern Pacific work clothes for her husband and other men. She washed them by hand on a washboard.

They moved again right after his mom passed away. Dad was only nine years old. We have one picture of our grandmother. To me, she looks Vietnamese but to others she looks more Yaqui, an Indigenous people and Native American tribe. We don't know much of her family history nor my Dad's father's side.

While Dad's mom was sick, he had the duty to care for her and his brothers. His dad could not help since he had an accident at Southern Pacific during work and lost his memory. I recall that the last time I saw him, he was sitting on a chair staring into space. He stayed with Dad's aunt until he passed away in December of 1967.

Dad's brothers were William, then Joe, and Alfred, the youngest. We knew Uncle Alfred and called him Uncle "A." He was in all our family celebrations.

They were eventually placed in foster homes, splitting the boys. There are stories of abuse from the foster parents, including living with an uncle who owned a restaurant and had the young brothers cleaning and sweeping the restaurant floors and cooking menudo on weekends and sometimes after drunken parties.

They lived in an attic with a metal roof. They were cold in the winter and hot in the summer. The family had another child and so they could no longer live there. They were eventually moved to a home with a foster mother who had other kids in her care.

Emilio, one of the foster siblings, stayed on with my father and his siblings and later became my Godfather. He and his family became our close friends. We saw his children as our cousins and the only cousins we knew from my dad's side. I was closer in age with Annie and Rose, Emilio's oldest daughters. I envied their beautiful long shiny hair. How I wished that when my hair grew, it would look just like that!

By this time, Dad had attended three elementary schools. He attended Safford Junior High and soon after moving in with Lupe, he decided to join the Army Air Force in 1944. He remembers when Pearl Harbor was attacked. He was sitting at a theatre when it was announced. All military persons were asked to return to base.

Dad's boot training was in Wichita Falls and from there he was transferred to New Jersey and later sent to Germany. He was sent on a mission to Dakar Africa and on the way, they had to land on water because of engine failure. They were on life rafts for more than six hours waiting to be picked up.

He visited Naples, Italy; Newfoundland; and Frankfurt, Berlin Germany. He was in the Army for six and a half years. In 1949, after being discharged in Pensacola, FL, he worked preparing materials to be shipped overseas. He re-enlisted in 1950 because of the Korean conflict and was discharged in 1953.

He returned to his foster home and traveled with his foster mother, Lupe. We called her Tía (aunt) Lupe because she was our mom's tía. She was related to our grandmother's side of the family.

Dad's upbringing had a lot to do with how he raised us. He was always on edge and mean at times, especially with Mom. He never physically abused her; it was verbal abuse. When we have conversations about him, we always circle back to his childhood. He was never a child. He had responsibilities as a child starting with caring for his mom. He had his brothers to worry about. He had school and his future to worry about.

Dad wanted us to have more than what he had, but for a long time he couldn't afford to give us more than the houses we lived in and the food we ate.

Dad as well as Mom didn't know how to show emotion or feelings nor were they affectionate. They didn't hug us nor tell us they loved us. The hugs came when we were older and moved out. When visiting, the hugs came when we arrived and hugs when we left. These hugs were passed on to anyone and everyone who walked into our home.

Mom in Hermosillo shopping - 19 yrs. old.

Mom in Hermosillo in her oxford shoes.

Mother

We know more of Mom's upbringing and so there is more to share. Her parents were stern and so Mom has been the strict one in our family. These are some stories of Mom and in some, I can see her clumsiness in me. As much as I don't want to be like her, I do find that I am feisty and as stubborn as she is. Mom is too honest in her opinions; I keep mine within, especially if they are hurtful. She is also very critical and tells us she speaks the truth. We try to convince her that she needs to think before she speaks. She could be hurtful sometimes.

Growing up, we were never given choices until we began to understand that we had other choices. We ate what we were served, we did what was asked and later for me, the career I wanted to pursue was squashed by her.

From so many years having Mom make my decisions, when I married, I let my husband do all the choosing of trips, colors of walls, colors of our cars, etc. One day I realized that he didn't care if I made the decision if the colors didn't go too wild! He tells me that intermixed patterns of bright colors make him dizzy. I'm the opposite, the more color and the brighter, the better — but I compromise. The pots I paint are bright. The quilts I make are colorful. The clothes I wear are yellows, oranges, and reds like the Tucson sunsets. The blues are like the ocean and the sky.

My mother, Teresa Granillo, was born on September 11, 1931, in Rayón, Sonora, Mexico, to Nana Anita Granillo and Ricardo Granillo (not related). She was a preemie baby. Her scheduled birth month was November, but she was born in September. She was laid in a dresser drawer that became her crib until she was too big to fit. She was breastfed but never ate enough. Even when growing up, she didn't like anything except the Saturday "raspados" (snow cones), that her dad bought her and her siblings!

Mom was one of six. Tío Manual was the only boy. The sisters are tías (aunts) and most go by nicknames: Tili (aka Matilde), Chata (aka Mariana), Chalita (aka Maria del Rosario), Fina (aka Josefina) and Amelia. We have a cousin also named Chalita. She

26

will not have the preceding "tía" since she is not our aunt but is very much part of the family. In our family, it is impolite to call an aunt by the first name without the preceding "tía"(aunt).

When Mom was old enough to go to school, she was excited that her best friend was going to start school with her but then disappointed when she found out that her friend would be a year behind. She told her friend, wanting to show off, "When I go to school, you are going to come looking for me to play and Mom is going to tell you that I'm at school."

She attended sixth grade three times because grades only went to sixth grade, and she was not able to leave for further education. She stopped repeating them when it was obvious that she was much older than the new kids coming in.

One day when they were out for recess, a teacher came out calling her in an angry tone,

"¡T E R E S A, ven aquí!" "Teresa, get over here!" She immediately ran to the office to find out what she did wrong. Turns out the teacher needed her to balance her books. Mom did very well in math. Even at 92, she can calculate her receipt faster than I can pull out my calculator.

Mom wanted to be in fashion, so she asked for a black and white pair of oxford shoes. They didn't have her size, so she took the smaller size and stuffed her feet in them until they wore out. I must agree that most women like to be in fashion and love to spend money on shoes.

Mom's friend, who worked with her at the "changarro" (convenience store), insinuated that Mom wasn't doing a great job in sewing her own dresses so referred her to Conchita, the town seamstress. When my sister, Ana was born, Conchita made her three dresses that she wore until the material wore out.

Mom also had chores at home. She didn't like taking part in making corn tortillas. To make corn tortillas they shucked the corn, washed it and left it overnight to dry. In the morning, they ground it and made the tortillas. They stuffed them with "nata" from the fresh morning's milk. Nana Anita (my grandmother) milked the cows early in the morning and made cottage cheese, but the top layer was the best and that is what is called the "nata."

Growing up, Mom was a disaster. She was nicknamed "forastera," meaning she was a visitor or an outsider, meaning she wasn't like her siblings. She shared some of her stories with us and some are too funny not to share!

One day the wood stove needed to be lit. It already had embers. She brought a can of kerosene and splashed some on the wood and it exploded. She burned her arms and hands, and Nana Anita didn't fuss about whether she was okay and instead had her proceed making the tortillas. Mom suffered from the burns but did not disobey her mom.

This is why Mom never fussed when we got hurt doing what we weren't supposed to be doing; instead, she told us to do it again. This is when I learned from her to be tough, experiencing it more later in life. I kept so much internally, and it was the wrong thing to do. When least expected, what was kept neatly in place came spilling out on a manager, my husband, siblings, or anyone who wanted to listen, or pretended to care and then I worried for having done so!

Another time, Nana Anita had labored over cleaning cotton bolls from the fields. The cleaned pieces of cotton lay by her feet. It was getting dark, so Nana Anita asked her to light the kerosene lamp. She lit it and dropped the match, yes right on top of the cleaned cotton bolls!

Another time after dinner, all the dirty dishes were stacked on the middle of the table. Mom was trying to fan a fly away with her hand and with her arm knocked down all the dishes. Her dad was there so her mom didn't scold her.

As much as I try to deny Mom's accusations of being clumsy or a troublemaker or being stubborn and hard-headed, I know I am, too, and as an adult I find myself doing dumb things. Just recently, I went to grab a plate for dinner and when I went to pick it up, I felt something hard and sticky. At first, I pulled back, thinking a dead animal then I slowly pulled it out to find a dirty dish from the night before. I blamed my husband knowing darn well it was me, and so I confessed. Once, I put leftovers in the cupboard and couldn't find them in the refrigerator. Then there have been countless times when cooking, I'll put my bare hand on the pan handle or grab a pan from the oven without mittens and scorch my hands.

Women try to do too many things at once and so I know that I become mindless, just going quickly from here to there and only satisfied when I sit down in the evening, and I can sigh with satisfaction that I have accomplished 95% of what was on my to-do list! Then I lay awake dwelling on the 5% I didn't get to.

Mom was healed by Saint Therese, as she tells us in this story. She had work done on a tooth and when done she was sent home from the dentist's clinic. She began to hemorrhage. She said the blood coming out of her mouth filled a small bucket. She was rushed to Hermosillo from Rayón. At that time, it was about a two-hour drive. The hospital did nothing for her other than to have her return to the dentist in Rayón. They went back and when she sat at the dentist chair she passed out and remembers Saint Therese brushing by her side and when she awoke the dentist told her there wasn't anything wrong. She went home and had a big meal, which is surprising since she was such a finicky eater.

When Mom told this story to my brother-in-law Phil (Ana's husband), he began calling her by "Nana Santa Teresita" (Grandma Saint Teresa). Now many refer to her this way, including Fr. Bardo, her spiritual son.

Mom celebrating her 92nd birthday – here with Fr. Bardo

Mom with her sisters – From back left, Fina, Chalita, mom, Tili, Chata, front is Amelia and Nana in the center.

Mom and Dad - December marriage in 1953 - (picture taken in Spring 1954).

Mom in beautiful wedding dress.

Parent's Marriage

It is such a contrast, having Mom proposed to within three months of dating and getting married within a few months after that and then beginning a family. Ralph and I dated for six years, married for six years before our daughter was born, mainly due to infertility problems. So, we literally had twelve years before we had our miracle baby. Our daughter, Melissa is now on the same track, but I'm hopeful it won't be for long.

Mom met our dad during Dad's travels with his foster mother, Tía Lupe. She had relatives in Rayón and Ures, so she took the boys on small vacations to visit her relatives. Dad's brother, uncle Alfred, fell in love with a lady from Ures. They invited Mom and her sisters to go to the wedding, where Dad danced with Tía Chata, her younger sister. Mom thought he was in love with Tía Chata, so she didn't give him any attention.

Later, after the wedding, Tía Lupe and the boys continued visiting. Dad made his stops at the changarro to buy cigarettes and to flirt with Mom. He finally asked her out and had dated for three months when he proposed to her. Mom quickly accepted.

Mom was the first one to get her marriage officiated by Fr. Sandoval. The wedding was in the late evening of December 27, 1953. Rayón didn't have electricity at that time, so lights from the farm trucks lit up the streets for the guests walking to church. Mom was in Dad's car. The church was lit with candles and in passing, Mom's veil caught on fire but was put out before it could spread. She later used the remaining veil to make small girl's veils for First Communions. Dad brought Mom to the U.S. early in 1954. Since they didn't take wedding pictures in Mexico, they had professional pictures done shortly after they moved to Tucson. She is wearing her bridal dress and veil, and both look so young and beautiful!

Family

"My family is my strength and my weakness.
—Aishwarya Rai Bachchan

D ad went back and forth from Tucson to Rayón. After Dad passed away, I was cleaning out his desk and found a folder with legal documents like their marriage certificate, Mom's passport, awards Dad received from his last employer and many more. Then I came across the document that had the Mexican and American official approvals to bring our mom into the U.S. legally. She moved to Tucson in April 1954 and began having our family, starting with Ana.

From this time, going forward, they had only one goal and it was our education. Of course, having shelter and food came first, but then it was education. They also wanted to keep us safe and out of trouble.

For a few years, we had to deal with Dad's moods. I was labeled the peace maker, always trying to get between Mom and Dad or between a sibling and Dad. Always trying to prevent the boat from rocking, trying to get ahead of the storm. I became a worrier, and I carried that worry throughout my life, in my career, in my activities and in raising my daughter. Worrying is exhausting!

Without their awareness, our parents taught us teamwork, they taught us to obey the law and to do things legally without taking shortcuts. They taught us discipline and they taught us to build and to break down and that it would be okay most of the time.

Mom helped raise the six children by earning extra income, sewing, and making tamales for various clients. She made school uniforms, bridal and quinceañera dresses. The extra income was to help pay for our Catholic education.

Quinceañera celebrations are like the American sweet sixteen celebrations, except it is when the young lady turns 15. When a young lady turns 15 in Mexico, she dresses in a dress resembling a bride's dress or a princess dress. Because of all the people invited to be part of the celebration, it looks like a wedding! The young girl dances the first dance with her dad. From this day forward, she may now participate in dating and dancing. Dating usually means having a chaperone.

My sisters and I had no desire to have a quinceañera celebration. Even later in life after we all had children, it was decided to have one big celebration rather than a quinceañera. Included were three nieces and one nephew, and my daughter, all who had birthdays around the same time. Mom made white satin dresses for the girls for this occasion but that is as close as it got to a typical quinceañera. The celebration was at our home and Fr. Bardo was the celebrant.

Ladies from the church learned that Mom was a seamstress. People brought Mom patterns and fabric and Mom turned the fabric into beautiful dresses. Some men brought slacks and shirts needing alterations. When she sewed, things got messy with pieces of fabric on the floor, along with thread, needles, and whatnot. She made sure we picked up after her and right before Dad, the inspector, came home from work. Eventually, it became a routine without Mom asking us to do so. While we picked up, she cooked his dinner that had to be ready by the time he sat down to eat, usually between 4:30 and 5:00 p.m....

I was very aware of my Dad's moods. I played the peace maker, protecting Mom from his harsh words. On the days he came home from work, after stopping for drinks with friends, he would come home in a rage. Once he threw his black lunch pail across the kitchen counter. If his dinner was not on the table, he'd have fits.

One day, he came in pretty wasted and went into the restroom slamming the door behind him. I started crying. I must have been about 8 or 9. When he came out, he saw me and asked why I was crying. I was afraid to answer him but finally blurted out that he was mean and scary and not nice to my mother. I think he was shocked that I spoke that many words at once. He put his hand on my shoulder and apologized. He promised me he would stop drinking. A few days later he was diagnosed with diabetes and was told to stop his drinking.

Sometimes Dad still showed his ugly side. He became irritated when clients came over for fittings. Mom worried so much and so then I worried. The person happily greeted Dad and Dad would force a greeting that was so obvious that he was being bothered. Mom quickly took them to the room where they tried on the dress. On their way out, Dad had moved himself away from their path and into the dining room where he peacefully drank his coffee and smoked.

One day, Mom told Dad, "I don't like how you treat the visitors. You know that the extra money I make is to send our kids to Catholic schools. If you don't want me sewing, then we will send them to the public schools." Mom wasn't afraid to speak up and when she did, her voice was calm and brave. Like her, it took a whole lot of pressure before I could speak up, but later in life I found the courage to speak sooner to avoid anger and resentment.

After that, if he knew a client was scheduled to appear for a fitting, he'd go into his bedroom or if it was a cool day, he'd sit on the back porch. This incident helped both Mom and Dad. Mom released tension and realized she had a voice, and Dad learned that his moods were too transparent. I truly believe this was the first time he was reprimanded in a respectable and loving way.

Not too much later, Mom also told Dad that one of the neighbors told her that her husband smokes outside because he respects and loves her. So, taking the hint, a few days later, Dad started smoking outside. He even had his last cigarette of the day outside before going to bed. Mom was getting assertive.

Mom was also employed by Ettore "Ted" DeGrazia, sewing sequins onto sweater designs. He paid her $1.00/hour. He was very cheap. Her friend took her to work and sometimes she continued sewing the sequins into the late evenings. This is the only time she ever worked outside of the house. Because she has only this incident of working outside of the home, she doesn't understand what it's like to be at work for 12+ hours, coming home to cook, clean, wash, and go through the mail, and preparing for the next day. She assumes we have energy left to go run her errands or go over to pick up the enchiladas she made us for dinner or whatever. I can't deny her, after all she went out of her way to cook extra to share with us. Her real reason, though, is to see us. We get busy with work and sometimes we could go days without visiting and the older she gets, the more she needs us.

Mom and Dad cried when John F. Kennedy was killed. They watched the landing of the moon in awe! These were the times we saw Dad's emotional side.

I remember my brother Richard was about seven years old when our parents' friend, Amparo, came to visit. She was commenting that walking on the moon was impossible and not true. Richard started arguing with her. "Why can't you believe it, because you didn't witness it?" She continued, saying, "Don't listen to that stuff, it's not true." Finally, frustrated and a little confused, Richard walked out, saying, "Then why is it that I believe you baptized me?" She was his Godmother, and he was baptized as an infant, as most Catholics are, so he trusted it was true. She was also the one who called me "Chiva."

She was also very much into politics. One year she brought Barry Goldwater to our home. He must have looked funny standing in our small living room.

It was the Spring of 1975 around the same time I began working at a car dealership, when Mom was certified by the State to care for children. Cynthia, our neighbor was a professor at the University of Arizona and was a single mom needing a licensed day care for her children. Dad filled out all the paperwork and later was visited to ensure the house had all the requirements. She was approved!

Our family almost always ate dinner together. The children Mom cared for loved it when Mom made tacos for dinner. Laurie made the salsa from fresh vegetables. She roasted the tomatoes on our gas stove burner, then peeled them and mashed them. She added cilantro, garlic, and the chili tepín peppers. It was delicious. We had contests as to who could eat the most tacos. Even today, tacos are the families' favorite meal.

Cynthia, the mother of the kids Mom cared for, became good friends of our family. She sometimes called on Dad to give rides to her kids to school or to some activity. He didn't like going out after working a full day so that put him in an ugly mood. During one of these requests, Dad was extremely put off and showed it. I was so angry and embarrassed and that same evening, I needed him to drive me to my evening job at the car dealership. I was a receptionist, sitting in the open, in the new car sales floor. He had no choice. He drove me in his old green truck. It made for a long drive from home. We didn't speak a word. When we got there, I jumped off and went straight in. About five minutes later, one of the salesmen comes over and says, "Go talk to your dad. He's waiting for you to say good-bye." I was being defiant, refusing to until it was becoming more embarrassing for the salesman to keep coming over to beg me to say good-bye to Dad, who wasn't going anywhere. I angrily stood up and walked outside. Dad had his window down, and I said, 'Thanks!" and marched back in, and Dad drove off. I felt bad and guilty, but all was back to normal when he picked me up at the end of my shift.

Dad also had a soft spot. When he punished us, we were sent to a corner, but it was just any wall, whichever was closest to him so he could watch. We had to face the wall for 10 to 15 minutes thinking about why we were there. When the time ended, he took us to the Dairy Queen for ice-cream. Mom would get so angry. Being strict, I was surprised she didn't stop Dad from the treats!

Mom had her faults too. When we cried, we were told to stop with the silliness. When we injured ourselves, she didn't come running to console us. When we came to give her good news of an accomplishment, it was not a big deal to her. She used to tell me to never think I was exceptional in anything because someone else will come along greater than me. Maybe that's why it is so hard for me to accept compliments. I would rather pay compliments a million times rather than receiving one. When I compliment people, I do it with all sincerity. I also compliment people who have hurt me because it's the current action I compliment, not the abrasive one.

Dad became more involved at St. John's Church. Both became Cursillistas. Cursillistas, as I understand, is a weekend couples' retreat. It is religious and very spiritually uplifting and I have witnessed many people change after the encounter. This is when Dad started to get more involved with church activities and his moods were changing for the better. It also meant more special services to attend, me included.

Easter was another holiday that involved an activity but for us, it was a holy event. During Holy Week, we had to attend the Holy Week services in the evenings, so we never watched television. We used to fight Mom and Dad over that, but they always won. One time it was raining hard, and I didn't feel well but I was forced to attend. While walking up the stairs at church, I slipped and fell hard on one knee. I was wearing boots and the fall caused them to rip right below the knee. I was fine, nobody fussed over me, and the knee healed on its own time.

When I was older, with one of my tía's help, we began to paint eggs and emptied out eggs to make "cascarones." These are hollowed eggs stuffed with confetti. The fun part was sitting at our dining room table as a family. Dad started participating more in our activities. We had all the supplies, such as newspaper, colorful tissue paper, homemade glue, scissors, and the eggs and confetti. We made papier mache cones out of the newspaper. While they dried, we cut strips of the tissue paper then cut ½ inch slits along the length and then curled the ends. When the cones dried, the strips were glued around the cone. On top of the cone, we glued the stuffed egg. On Easter, the eggs are popped on people's heads!

This whole process in making the beautiful "cascarones" as a team, reminds me of one of my last experiences at a company that was bought out by a larger company. We were to build our own system and so we were teamed with developers and business analysts. We worked hard creating and testing and spending lots of money. At the end, they decided they would keep their own system. So just like that, all the hours and effort and money went down the drain. It's like the "cascarones" that are meticulously decorated only to be shattered within seconds with a pop on a head.

I also introduced my younger siblings to Halloween costumes and Easter egg hunts. Our parents weren't interested in Halloween, much less making costumes for their kids. So, when I was old enough to create costumes out of whatever we had at home, I made up costumes for the boys, Laurie, and myself. I either walked with them, or they joined neighbor friends. I still dress in a Halloween T-Shirt or a full costume when at work for our costume contest. I then leave it on until late, after helping Mom with the Trick or Treaters.

Mom was very devoted to praying the rosary and still is. In May, she made us go to church to offer flowers to the Virgin Mary and pray the rosary. We had a neighbor that invited us to cut flowers from her beautiful garden of roses, carnations, and snap dragons. The smell of carnations and roses always take me back to these times.

The routine was picking the flowers, getting to church with Dad or a neighbor. We lined up at the back of the church. There were usually about 10 kids, girls, and boys. We walked into church in a procession. We were all seated at the front pews of one side of the church. There was a friend of Mom's, who sat behind us to ensure we didn't misbehave. We got the eye if we talked or giggled or need to be shushed to keep quiet. Mom sat away from us, which was good, otherwise she would be pinching our arms if she caught us goofing off.

One Sunday, when we all went to church, Ana sat next to me. There was some commotion and Mom thought Ana and I were giggling when she saw me lying on the bench. She was about to grab my arm, probably to pinch it, when she realized I had fainted. We never knew the cause.

Mom also attended daily mass as often as she could, especially first Fridays and Saturdays of the month. This required Dad to drive her to church until she met women who befriended her and offered to pick her up.

In December 1978 she became the Deacons wife. Dad was in training to become a Catholic Deacon and after 4 years he was ordained for the "Permanent Diaconate". He was appointed to exercise the ministry at St. John's the Evangelist Church. He was allowed to assist at marriages and officiate baptisms and was required to prepare the homily and present it to the church congregation. The Deacon's wife's role is to support her husband. Mom was supportive of Dad but also worried. She always worries about what others may think. Dad's Spanish was not perfect, so when he had to write and read the homily in Spanish, she got sick with worry that he would mis-pronounce words. The night before, he studied by reading out loud and Mom corrected him each time he mispronounced a word. I always worried that he would snap at any moment from being corrected.

On May 25, 1987, Mom became a US Citizen. Because she didn't speak much English, Dad asked to go as a translator, but was not allowed. When she was done, Judge Sandra Day O'Connor told Dad that Mom had done an excellent job on her own!

In 2002 they moved from the home they lived in for 45 years. My husband and I had been gone for over 20 years, living in

San Diego, then Colorado. It was in 2001, that we moved from Colorado back to Tucson when my sisters mentioned that they were trying to convince Dad to move closer to Laurie's home and the house we moved into. Both houses are in the Northwest side of Tucson. They were to move from the South side. Dad was not liking any of it. I talked to Dad and convinced him to move. Mom had already decided years earlier, but she needed Dad to make the decision.

Laurie had already seen a house she thought they would like. Mom fell in love with the back yard. It has two big grapefruit trees, beautiful rose bushes, and a big jacaranda (aka black poui) tree. When it blooms, you can see beautiful purple flowers from blocks away. The backyard also had a white picket fence separating part of the yard. The bonus was that it was within walking distance to a Catholic church.

They moved into this house shortly after viewing it and Mom began walking to St. Elizabeth Ann Seton for daily mass, meeting many new friends.

They missed their Lincoln neighbors and friends. Dad especially missed sitting on the front porch smoking his cigarettes and waving at the neighbors. One of the neighbors told my parents that they were going to become snotty because they were moving to the rich side of town (it's not) and now most have moved out of the old neighborhood.

Sometime between the old house and the new one, Mom and Dad had the opportunity to travel to pilgrimages, but Dad never wanted to go, so he sent Mom with the church groups.

The first trip was a big surprise because Mom was so afraid of heights. She refused to go up "A" Mountain. It is more of a hill than a mountain. When we took her to Mt. Lemmon, she almost had a heart attack. So now she was flying!

Her first trip was to Medjugorje Bosnia and Herzegovina – Our Lady of Medjugorje She brought each of her kids and one for their home a big crucifix about 15" x 9". I don't know where she carried 7 of these crucifixes. Maybe it was miraculous.

Her next trip was to Mexico City to see the Basilica of our Lady of Guadalupe in Tepeyac Hill, Mexico City. On this trip, she and one of her friends separated themselves from the group. They wanted to go shoe shopping. When they were to return to the hotel, they had no idea where to start. They didn't know the name of the street nor remembered the hotel name. They went back into the shoe shop and asked for help. The man trying to help them kept asking for some clue to their destination. Finally, another man walked in and overheard them. "Ah, these ladies are with the church group! I think they are staying at the Hotel... (and mentioned the correct name)!" Mom and her friend were guided by an angel, they say when they tell the story.

The very next day, the priest decided to play a joke on them. Everyone else was in on the joke. There was an old taxi outside the hotel. It was there for looks and advertising the taxi service. Father had someone tell Mom and her friend to meet them at the taxi that was to drive them to their next destination. They didn't want to be late since they had already suffered humiliation from the day before and felt guilty for making the rest of the group worry about them. So, they hopped into the taxi and sat waiting for the taxi driver. They were into conversation when suddenly the group begins to surround the taxi and they are all laughing. They finally figured out that the taxi was there for show!

The next trip was to visit Our Lady Mary, Regina del Cielo in Finca Betania, Venezuela. The only comment on this trip was that it was beautiful and very green. The people were also very nice!

So, this woman who is afraid of heights and worried about everything decides to go on all these trips without a family member. She was feeling the same freedom that I felt while away at work and earlier in Rayón. To me, it was a freedom to be me and not the person who is constantly being told who to be.

Last family picture taken at mom's 90th birthday celebration – 2021.

Grade School

"The beginning is the most important
part of the work." —Plato

Grade school was one of my first formal and public exposures. If I hadn't had Ana as an older sister, I would have been in trouble. She's the one who explained what to expect on my first few days. She couldn't hold my hand throughout the school year, but I think I did okay on my own.

I understood our name-changes from the nuns.

Sisters and nuns are the female equivalent to a Friar and a Monk. In the past, women who chose to become a nun, entered a convent as a novitiate and known as a novice. They spent a year dedicated to prayer and learning the vows of a nun while focusing on religious life and the spirit of the community they have entered. Today, it is preferred that a sister receives a bachelor's degree but not a requirement. Once they have gone through their formal training, they go out into the world to serve. Some remain in their community or convent to pray and work, depending on the order.

Our sisters were from the order of Sisters of Charity, founded by St. Elizabeth Ann Seton in 1809. Their purpose was to work for the poor at hospitals, orphanages, elementary and secondary schools, and colleges.

We always referred to the sisters at St. John the Evangelist School as "nuns", but the formal reference should be by their given name such as "Sister Mary Antoinette" (my first-grade nun).

I understood the consequences for not completing my homework.

We wore uniforms so I didn't need to worry about what I wore, nor would I be criticized for not wearing the latest style. We all looked the same.

In grade school, I received scrapes and bruises, not just physically but mentally. Here are some examples:

In third grade, with prescription glasses came headaches before the diagnosis and later when I was being teased for wearing them.

In fourth grade, I was humiliated for not knowing American music.

In fifth grade, I was humiliated again for passing love notes.

The summers were with neighbors and Christmas was with family and then visiting friends with children who received much nicer gifts. I don't recall envy at all, just fantasizing having the same toys to play with at home, especially the Barbies and everything that goes with them.

One day, I fell going home from school and had to be carried home.

Richard having coffee with Mom and tattling on me about the milk I gave him at lunch.

I listened to parents arguing over the check-book balance.

Learning after the fact that our food was subsidized with food bags/baskets. Small staples but perhaps things my parents couldn't afford.

Diving off into an 8-foot pool and seeing Dad's white legs. These didn't cause pain, just giggles and laughter.

And here is more of what I remember and what I felt and how I didn't yet long to be anything or anyone else. I was my parents' child.

I entered grade school in 1962. I had just turned 6. Dad filled out all the paperwork since Mom didn't know English. He was also the one to read notes sent by the teacher. He enrolled us with our birth names, but the nuns Americanized our names.

In school, Ana's name changed to Anna (pronounced Anna like in banana). The correct pronunciation is like saying <u>"Aw nah"</u>. A few years ago, Ana began correcting anyone who called her by Anna and explained that her name is Ana.

My name was changed to match the other Sylvia in my class, "Silvia" with the "I" to replace the "y." My passport is with the "y" and so is my driver's license. One time I traveled out of the country, and I was required to show my birth certificate, the difference in spelling was questioned. Worse, Dad could never spell my name. He spelled it "Slyvia." It's a good thing he didn't pronounce it that way!

Laurie's birth certificate name is "Laura". We don't remember if her name was also changed at school and found out when applying for the University. We called her by "Laurie". I still can't call her by Laura unless I am referring to her in Spanish. My poor Mom couldn't pronounce it, so the younger brothers were always teasing her, "Loorriii," she would say!

Since Mom was the strict one, I feared her the most when it came to confrontations. She was also a stay-at-home Mom. She inspected what we wore and what we ate. She fought us with breakfast, especially me. I didn't want to eat, I just wanted to be at school as quickly as possible. To solve that problem, she made us what she called "ponche." It turns out to be a semi-healthy milkshake. She made it with a scoop of ice-cream followed by a raw egg and a drop of coffee, and a drop of milk and blended it. We loved it even though it wasn't the healthiest drink right before school.

Ana didn't know she was my role model. I watched how she dressed. Later in life, I liked going shopping with her. A memory that I am sure all little girls have, is that the night before, we laid out our uniform, socks, and underwear. We pulled out the best underwear without holes in case we fell, per Mom and all mothers. When we had brand new undies, and socks, we loved the smell of the brand-new material! For us it was mainly right before the new school year and maybe for Christmas.

The first episode for me was in first grade with Sister Mary Antoinette. She was usually nice but on this one day, I had forgotten to do my homework, so she made me stay in during lunch to complete it. I was so embarrassed and worried that I might not get to eat my lunch. I know I suffered for the first 15 minutes that seemed like eternity. She had left the classroom to check on the other students. When she returned, she told me I could eat my lunch. I never again forgot to do my homework!

In second grade, Richard, our neighbor, and my friend, made our First Communion with me. Mom made my white dress and veil. I remember the brand-new white vinyl prayer book and rosary tucked inside in a tiny plastic bag. We carried it as we walked in procession to the front pews. My hair was in curls and still a red color. In a picture I have, it appears that I am frightened or extremely shy.

I don't recall anything else that happened at school until the third grade when we discovered I needed prescription glasses and being bullied about being a four-eyed monster.

It was fourth grade when I won a spelling bee that I won't ever forget. Growing up at home, we didn't listen to music. If we did, it was Mexican music, or the quiet music Dad played every single night. The station was KAIR or CAIR. Whatever the name, it was like elevator music. One of my tías and my dad played their Mexican music on weekends. I learned some of the lyrics and when I was older and spent time in Rayón, I listened to even more Mexican music. It wasn't until Ana was in high school that our neighbor, Mario, shared some albums with her. Then when she worked, she started buying the albums and that's when I was introduced to American artists. Laurie, on the other hand, remembers more American music so it seems that the years between us and hanging out with friends who listened to American music made the difference. Laurie also didn't spend as much time in Mexico as I did. I didn't know who the Beatles were, nor did I know Elvis Presley. I recall my friends going crazy over the Beatles. I felt out of place.

So, I win this spelling bee. The teacher, this time not a nun, is at the front of the classroom announcing the prize and I'm wanting to hide.

"Sylvia, you won! What 45 record do you want? I will buy any song you choose." I was wishing I had not won. I had no idea who or what to pick. The girl behind me finally whispered, "Little Green Apples." And so that is what squeaked out of my mouth.

In about the fifth or sixth grade, I was caught passing notes with Michael. We used to like each other, so instead of listening to the teacher, we were busy writing love notes. The teacher, who was a nun, took the note away and told us, "Pay attention. Your parents will be called."

All I could think about was Dad getting the phone call. Sure enough, in the evening when the nun knew he'd be home, she called. The phone rings and I'm walking outside pretending it was just any phone call. A few minutes later, Dad calls me inside with Mom next to him.

"What were you doing in class today? Do you have a boy-friend?" I tell him, "It was Michael and, no, he's not my boyfriend." He had a smile all this time. Mom was the one upset and embarrassed about the call. I was not reprimanded, just told to not distract the class with silliness. I was so relieved!

My parents didn't teach us anything about our bodies, much less sex! Instead, they had an encyclopedia opened to the biology of the body on the coffee table. Remember the one with the clear plastic with different body parts? Each overlay of the plastic created different parts of the body.

In sixth or seventh grade, a few of us were goofing off during lunch and a boy fell on top of me and stayed on top of me a little longer than he should have. For the next week I worried that I was pregnant. How naïve!

During the primary years, we carpooled with the neighbors. Mr. or Mrs. Gonzales drove us to school. Veronica was a year behind me, and we were friends. Between both families we had older siblings who walked home with us. It was a mile walk. At first there was no overpass, so we had to cross the freeway. If it rained, Mrs. Gonzales picked us up, or we walked across the street to the house where Dad caught his carpool.

Dad parked his car at a woman's house that was right across from our school. We stopped at the Circle K on our way to her house and bought candy. We also loved the saladitos (dried plums or apricots coated with salt and hot spices). We ate them with lemon, a lemon with a saladito stuffed in the middle. We always ate the candy before Mom caught us. We walked over to the woman's house and waited for Dad in her living room. I don't know who this woman was, but she was always nice to us.

When the construction began on I-10, an overpass was added, so that we no longer needed to cross the highway. We were lazy and continued taking the old route until one day, some guys that were walking on the overpass spit down on us and on another occasion, we had soda poured on us. We decided the overpass was safer. Sometimes to take the overpass we took the quick route that meant walking through a very rocky wash and walking down the embankment supporting the new overpass. We were on our way home, and we decided to go down the embankment. I slipped and fell landing on top of the rocks in the wash. Selma, the oldest of the Gonzales girls, had to carry me home. Thank goodness I was okay, but Mom freaked out. I got to see her face when she saw me. I couldn't tell if she was mad or worried but it kind of made me feel special.

Since we didn't have much money to spare, we watched the other kids at school as they ate their Popsicles. There was a day in the week when the school provided Popsicles or ice-cream cups for 10 cents. Occasionally, if we found change under the couch cushions or under the car mats, we were lucky and bought our own Popsicle!

We didn't have fancy book bags or later, backpacks. We had to take a quarter to school to buy a cheap clear plastic one that the school bought in bulk. We also had to cover our textbooks to keep them clean. We watched some students with colorful covers but some of us used the brown heavy grocery bags. We decorated them with Crayolas.

The school offered milk at lunch. Dad paid it monthly or yearly. We took our lunches but drank the school milk except for me. I gave mine to Richard. Each time I'd tell him not to tell Mom. I didn't like the milk and later found out I am lactose intolerant.

In the summers, Richard came to our house looking for me to play or to get me to go outside to play at his house. I always slept in, so Richard waited with Mom. Mom made him a cup of coffee, but it was really milk with a tiny bit of coffee. Mom had hers. They were pals and during one of these visits, he told Mom about my milk! Mom made me feel guilty, by telling me, "¡Tu padre trabaja duro para que tengan comida, y tú la das!" Your Dad works hard to buy you food and you give it away!"

The rest of grade school was uneventful, other than having problems learning. Dad got frustrated with me when I'd get his help at night but not as impatient as he was with Jerry when it was his turn to go to school. He couldn't learn his colors. Dad would say, "What color is the curtain? And he'd say, "blue" but it was green. "What color is the chair? He'd say, "Green" but it was blue.

During the summers of my primary years, we played with our neighbors. We rode our bicycles until dusk and then either Mom or Dad called us in. I played with Veronica when Richard wasn't around. We climbed up her plum tree and ate them before they ripened. To keep us from eating them, our moms told us we would get diarrhea.

When Veronica came to our house, we pretended to fly by jumping off our couches and then we would giggle. Veronica had a good strong, loud laugh and so she would get me going, too. Mom was always pregnant and when she tried resting and especially when it was a nap she needed, she took it before Dad came home. When we laughed, she yelled at us from the bedroom to be quiet. "Se ríen sin ganas!" She was saying we were force-laughing or laughing for no reason.

Sometimes Mr. Gonzales took us to the Country Club pool. I never learned how to swim but I was never afraid to dive into the 8-foot section of the pool. Today, I would not attempt it! The first-time dad went with us, we giggled to see him in trunks and seeing his white legs for the first time! He never wore shorts.

Richard's family owned a color TV so when the Wizard of Oz was shown, they invited us over to watch it with them. Laurie came along since Anna Marie, Richard's sister, and Laurie were in the same grade and best friends. Laurie didn't hold back her tears. I think she only went one time.

Richard's mom, Terry, loved me. She always knew what I liked to eat and what I couldn't eat. When she gave her kids birthday parties, she either ordered a cake or baked a cake. If the cake of choice was coconut, she baked a separate white cake just for me! She also knew that Mom forbade us from eating sweets and drinking soda pops. She never bought them, and I always thought it was because they couldn't afford unnecessary things. Later, the boys did get their Ding Dongs, and Twinkies! Probably more because Dad loved them and took one or the other in his lunch box. If Terry wanted to give us any of those forbidden sweets, she called Mom to get permission. Mom always approved because she knew it was just a one-time treat!

Christmas was a poor holiday for us, although we didn't know it until much later. Mom hated all the fuss made with decorating. Dad bought us a "Charlie Brown" tree. We had very little decorations. It was mostly filled with tinsel. As we worked and earned money, the tree became bigger and more beautiful, but Mom was still not a happy lady. She said it was because Dad always got into his moods and plus, in Mexico when growing up, they didn't go through all the trouble in decorating, and it was more about Jesus than the commercial stuff! When she was growing up, she and her siblings received a stocking filled with an orange and loose candy and nuts. That was all. It was placed on the pillow or on their side as they slept.

The tradition in our home was that we first drove our parents crazy with the anticipation of Christmas Eve when we opened our gifts. Mom and sometimes one of our aunts made tamales on the day of Christmas Eve and sometimes until late at night. In the evening after dinner, Mom sat in the living room, with a stack of unfinished dresses. She was sewing the hem or adding the last button. These were the dresses we wore to mass on Christmas morning.

We were sent to bed to take a nap. I liked to lay on our parent's bed. As I lay in bed, I focused on a picture frame with a 3D image of the Virgin Mary and depending how I looked at it, Jesus appears. The frame had a green or blue Christmas light bulb shining on the picture. The light made the picture look more vivid, and I waited to see if it would come to life. I fell asleep before it did. Such an imagination!

We woke up to a happy Dad. He was now so proud and happy of the few little gifts that Santa brought us. We sat in the living room on the cold floor. It was either a new baby doll or hair accessories and new clothes for me. Ana received some educational toy or book and new clothes, and occasionally a doll. Laurie was gifted dolls and new clothes.

Later in the afternoon we visited friends. Mom gifted them with tamales. If the family had children, we listened to the kids talk about the gifts they received. Sometimes we played in their rooms and saw a new record player, a stack of 45's and Barbie dolls. The new gift was the Barbie car or house and many Barbie clothes. I inspected the beautiful Cinderella dresses so that one day I could take Mom's scraps and sew new dresses for my dolls. As we got older, we went to the midnight mass and the routine changed, but not by much.

We didn't know what little we had. I was recently reminded by Laurie that Mom received a food bag filled with food such as powdered milk, rice, a block of cheese and some vegetables. There was also a neighbor who worked at Hostess Bread. She was the one who brought us day-old bread and later donuts. Later, Dad took us to the Hostess Bread store to buy the day-old Twinkies and Ding Dongs.

I know that at some point the food bags stopped because Dad began driving Mom to do the grocery shopping. He either sat in the car or drove back home and waited for her call. And the other reason is because Mom always forgot to write the amount in the check book and threw the receipt away. When Dad tried balancing the checkbook against the bank statement, he would get angry when something was missing. Sometimes I truly believed that Mom was the one who caused Dad to get into his moods. I didn't like it when he accused her of buying too much food. She later told him that the food was mainly what he wanted to eat: meats, potatoes, beans, and his oatmeal and eggs with toast in the morning.

Sylvia and Richard (neighbor) - First Communion.

Mom with Terry, Richard's mom, who made me special cakes.

Entertaining, Rayón and New Family Member

> *"The bond that links your true family is not one of blood, but of respect and joy in each other's life."*
> **—Richard Bach**

We did anything to keep Dad in a good mood. It meant choreographing plays, singing with or without the old guitar and keeping a routine, especially on Sundays. I didn't realize then that by creating these plays, I was beginning to form my creative side. I was learning to write, although not literally written in paper and pen but it was the formation of a script written into my memory.

When not trying to keep the family peace, I went to Rayón and learned that I was stuck between English and Spanish, affecting my reading. Going to Mexico was a different world. There were people who had less than us. My cousins were all in good homes — maybe not overflowing in wealth, but they lived comfortably. It was the other families who lived in huts or small adobe homes with dirt as their floor. I loved taking them our hand-me-downs. Now I was on the other side, and I was for once experiencing having more.

Math was also a weakness for me but had nothing to do with language. At this young age, I had no desire to use math, nor did I dream that someday my career would involve math that would affect a person's pay. I was innocent and didn't understand the value. Even if I understood the value, I eventually learned that the reason for my life was to be knowledgeable in helping others, serving others, befriending the odd ones, and loving even those who didn't like me. I was learning to love what I do and becoming aware of my actions and service to others and to giving credit where credit is due — including with thyself.

Staying in Mexico during the summer and listening only to Mexican music caused me to miss out on the excitement my school mates were having over Elvis Presley then the Beatles. I don't regret missing out and sometimes feeling left out because had it not been for the Mexican music, perhaps I would have never found the love of dancing Ballet Folklórico. The music also allowed me to let go on the dance floor at weddings and other Mexican festivities or like Bea, my sister-in-law, has taught me the freedom to dance in my kitchen or wherever I desire! If no one wants to participate, we go at it alone.

Good news when Tía Amelia married Bud, he became our second father role model with different views and opportunities that lifted us up. Sometimes it takes an outsider to point out flaws, in a kind way. Uncle Bud did just that. He also picked me out of my sisters to work with him and to accompany him into Mexico as a translator when he was looking for a specific car part or selling car parts. I didn't know anything about car parts in English, much less in Spanish.

This is the beginning of learning new tasks that I didn't seek but had pushed on me. I say that in a good way.

Buying new grown-up eyeglasses this time, I was not worried about the bullies.

Plays, Music, and Laughter

We entertained our parents to make them laugh and to keep the peace. I was the choreographer. I called on Laurie, Anna Marie, and sometimes Richard to be part of the cast. My younger brothers were too young to participate. They just got in the way. We dressed in our parents' clothes or found fabric to wrap around our bodies as costumes. We used ribbons that we found in Mom's sewing boxes. The girls wrapped them around their heads to look like princesses.

When we had rehearsed the play, we invited Terry, our neighbor and her kids and the rest of our family. Tía Amelia lived with us, so she was always part of the audience. They sat in the backyard on the dining room chairs and the benches from the picnic table. They placed them right in the middle of the yard. We were closer to the clothesline so we could use it for our props. We threw a sheet over the line to make it look like a background wall.

This time, we dressed like our parents and performed a day at the Roche's, except we were royalty. I dressed as an old lady. I wore one of Mom's dresses and stuffed the insides with whatever I could find. My stomach was a small pillow to look pregnant. I walked around as if in pain from the pregnancy. Richard was the dad. We played house and used dolls as our babies. Anna Marie and Laurie were our older children. I don't recall how the play went but the audience cheered and oh did they laugh! This was my creativity taking form with the help of my cast members.

Dad loved our humor and decided to play a prank on us. He surprised us one day as we were all sitting in the living room. He came walking down the hallway wearing a dress and high-heeled shoes. His feet weren't quite in the shoe. He was mimicking the ladies who came for fittings. We laughed, even Mom couldn't stop laughing but I knew she was the happiest seeing he was having fun! Watching Dad do this, helped me see that I could be silly, not caring what others think. Later in life, I realized where I got my silliness from. Even in the workplace, I have played jokes on others or randomly laughed at the silliest things, sometimes one of those non-stop laughter. Best of all, I've learned to laugh at myself, and I do that often.

Other entertainment came when Tía Amelia brought out her guitar. She was taking lessons but also pretended she could play it well and would sing "On Top of Old Smokey" for starters and as the night progressed the music turned to Mexican songs. In later years at any gathering with the Cursillistas, the men and women who participated in the Cursillo weekend retreat, sang the retreat's theme song, De Colores.

On Sundays, we began the tradition of having fried chicken. The neighbors did the same. Richard's house would start. We could smell the chicken, then Mom was next and soon the air in the neighborhood smelled like fried chicken! Later, as we got older and Dad was earning more and the kids were pitching in, it was "carne asada," steaks on the grill. I look back and think how interesting that we all make routines.

We make our routines at home, routines at work. Babies have their routines. The older we get, the more routines we make. I wish I could say I'm a spontaneous person but I'm not. There are reasons. First, I'm always caught in the middle of a creative project or work or mother caregiving, or secondly, we already have family plans. The Roche clan always has something going on. One day, I showed Bea our calendar to prove that we literally have events scheduled months in advance, birthday parties, weddings, baptisms, First Communions, graduations, funerals, etc.... At some point, we become immune and just go with the flow. My husband, Ralph, and I pretend we have this long list that we check off after an activity. We pull into our garage and say "Check, another one down."

Middle School

Middle school was at the same school as grade school at St. John's! We were now the older kids. We had more homework and at home more chores! The nuns were stricter on the length of our uniforms. If the uniform looked too short, they had us put our arms down with fingers stretched out. If the hem was shorter than our middle finger, we were sent to the office. I don't recall if they provided us with used uniforms or if they made us go home. I was never one of them! I finally did something right or I should say that it was because Mom inspected us before the nuns did!

There was a family that helped our family out by taking me to Girl Scout meetings and events. I went to their house after school on the days of the meetings. We were served graham crackers and milk, something I never had before. I'm surprised I had the milk there but not at school. This was a very nice gesture, and I will always remember those days.

We didn't invite our friends to have cookies or empanadas but later when I began working, I invited co-workers to have Mom's beans and tortillas. They loved this simple meal, especially if it was their first.

There was another incident I will always remember. This one is somewhat embarrassing. I must have been in the seventh grade. We were intently listening to our teacher giving us instructions on our homework, when a girl sitting in front of me sneezed and startled me. It was very loud, and I would have ignored it, but I heard a giggle from a boy sitting across from me and I got going and could not stop laughing. It was one of those uncontrollable laughs. The football nun was at the front of the room teaching until she heard me laughing. She was very tall and walked with long strides and was very strict and so she was named "the football nun." She marched right up to my desk and looked down at me and asked, "Sylvia, can you share the joke with the class?" I couldn't answer right away and finally blurted that it wasn't a joke.

"Then what is it, Sylvia?" she said. I kept laughing and the students next to me started laughing. The nun made all of us stop the laughter by threatening to make us stay in after school. I didn't stop until the girl in front of me turned around and I saw how red she had turned. I slowly stopped and at this time the nun had already started walking toward the front. Sometimes I wondered if God made me silly, clumsy, and naïve just to make people laugh, especially Dad. People laughing at me came soon enough.

Tía Amelia with my sisters Ana and Laurie – Celebrating Tía Amelia's graduation earning her degree as a Licensed Practical Nurse.

Tía Amelia

During my school summers, I spent weeks at a time in Rayón. I loved getting away from home. Tía Amelia lived with us, and she is the one who took us.

It is important to explain who Tía Amelia is and how she came to stay in our lives. She is one of Mom's younger sisters. She came to live at our house when Mom gave birth to our brother, Richard. She helped Mom and then later found work babysitting neighbor children and continued living at our home. She helped us with the heavy cleaning on weekends. She and my dad got along so much better than he and Mom, so that helped. She was the buffer between the two.

Tia Amelia was around 15 years old when she came to the United States. After her first babysitting job, she was referred to the Malloy family. They were looking for a nanny. The dad was a judge. The newborn needed a nanny. His older siblings were already in school, and the mom was busy with other matters. Tía Amelia became the nanny and was with them through all their lives. She had her own bedroom and bath. She came home on weekends. If the parents went on vacation, she spent the nights to care for the kids.

Because of Tía Amelia's work with the Malloys, we learned about entertaining. She was called to help prepare for big parties with important people. She took Laurie to help and for big parties, I was included. We had simple tasks such as removing the melted wax from small vases used as decorations at the last party and to be used for the next party. We also helped with anything they thought we could handle. We saw the many yummy dishes they served. For us everything was new and exciting. They had refrigerators in their large kitchen that looked like a regular cabinet. Wooden fronts and many layers for storing all the prepared dishes. Once we learned how to chop vegetables the right way or mastered the dusting, Laurie and I went more often. We took the bus from near St. John's church, and it dropped us off very close to where they lived. We came home with our pockets filled with our pay. Not only were we paid well, but we learned how to take direction and we observed, learned, and showed we could do the small tasks that for us were monumental at that time.

Tía Amelia also took us, where Dad didn't, like to the movie theatres, mainly to watch Mexican movies. One of the times Laurie cried throughout the movie. It was about a little girl who was kidnapped and kept in a cave. It went something like that. The movie isn't what I remember — but the hot dog we ate. We ordered a plain hot dog and we loaded ours with mustard and ketchup and tons of jalapeños. That was before the Sonoran dogs became popular. They were the best!

Tía Amelia began taking English classes and then began school at Pima Community College where she earned her Licensed Practical Nurses' degree. By this time the last child was going to school, so she was not needed full-time. She graduated and began working at a Nursing Home.

She was also my role model. The love she had for her work made it seem that work was going to be a fun adventure. I didn't know yet what I wanted to be when I grew up, but I had the desire to be important to someone. She was important to the mother of the children. The patients at the nursing home needed her and many were so appreciative of her dedication. In her later years, she was frustrated with the new hires right out of college. Many were lazy and didn't want to do the dirty work. Once she walked into a patient's room to find that the woman's food was placed on the hospital bed tray, but the table was never moved close to her. She sat staring at her food. She received awards for her timeliness, never missing work and for compliments she received from the patient's families.

My 13th Birthday Party

The summer when I turned 13 was the first party my parents gave me. I knew they didn't have the money for anything fancy and I also knew that Dad was excited to allow me this celebration. I was thrilled to invite my classmates. Since my birthday was right after school ends, I took the invitations to school and passed them out to the girls on our last day of school.

I helped clean the house and decorated with what we had. Mom baked the cake and bought pretty plates. I asked for pink forks because that's what Terry bought for her parties. Everything looked nice. The only thing is no one had called to advise they were coming.

On the day of my party, we waited and waited for someone to show up. No one showed up. My dad looked more disappointed than Mom. I was devastated and hurt but I kept it in. I didn't want to make it worse for Dad and Mom. The family celebrated with me. The excuse is that most families left town on vacation. Most parents took their kids to San Diego or were celebrating Father's Day. My birthday lands on Father's Day on some years. It is a busy week so I can see why no one came. When I turned 30, I threw my own party in San Diego and again when I turned 60 and both were a success.

Learning disappointment from my parents' side and then from being the recipient taught me that at some point in life there would be many more disappointments — and I was right.

My 60th birthday celebration (June 2016).

Welcome sign with my cousin Matilde.

Virgen de Guadalupe painted on rocks.

Rayón, Sonora

"You will never be completely at home again, because part of your heart always will be elsewhere. That is the price you pay for the richness of loving and knowing people in more than one place."
—Miriam Adeney

Long before Tía Amelia married her first husband, Bud, she was the one who drove us to Rayón to drop us off at our grandmother's home. Either Tía Amelia or our dad returned weeks later to pick us up. These long stays were during our summer breaks from school. Most of the time, I was the only one who stayed but only once Mom and Dad felt confident, I wasn't going to be trouble.

Going to Rayón and being left alone was freedom! It wasn't just a vacation from having to do chores at home but a freedom to be someone else. A place where I discovered another part of me. Yes, I still had grandparents and tías to obey but that was so minimal. The rest of the time was being with my cousins. Doing what a kid likes to do and later what teen-agers like to do. I didn't compare myself to anyone. I could come and go from my grandparents' house pretty much at any time of the day. I learned

66

new things and then surprised my parents when I returned from these trips. Sometimes I shared funny stories and sometimes bad things that I should have just kept to myself.

The excitement to go to Rayón wiped away the disappointment from the party that never happened. The drive to Rayón at that time, took about six or seven hours. Once we turned off the main road, the roads became dirt and rocky. We were prepared to put on our scarves to keep the dust out of our hair. It was about two hours of dust and bumps. Going through Carbo, it was rockier and longer, but it got us to the port right after crossing the river. Today, the roads are paved, making it a much quicker and smoother drive.

From the port, we could see the whole town. It is a valley dressed in green with a river flowing on the outskirts that continues south. This same river is the one we need to cross to continue to the port. There have been times when the heavy rains caused the river to overflow and there was no way to cross it other than by horse.

Looking down, the first thing you see is the steeple of the big white Catholic church, the only church that exists in the town. It is named "La Señora del Rosario" (Lady of the Rosary). If we keep looking to the east toward the last street, we could see my grandparents' home. At the forefront is the school that Mom attended. It has since been enlarged and modernized. Another addition, beyond the port there is a hill with a statue of the "Virgin de Guadalupe". I have not seen the improvements in person.

Then we begin looking at the houses, looking for our grandparents' house. What makes the sight so beautiful is that most houses are decorated with bright pots of flowers everywhere. My grandmother's backyard was always full of plants and beautiful flowers. The well sat off to the right side of the garden next to a huge mulberry tree.

The streets are named based on the status of the people living there but also at what point of the hilly land they are situated. This is what I understand: "Calle de Abajo" (street below or lower grounds). It means middle class. "Calle de Arriba" (upper street, or higher grounds). These are bigger houses, and some families own their own convenience stores or grocery stores. "Calle del alto" (high street or highest grounds). Same as Calle de Arriba. Then there is "El Bajio," (low land or the lowest grounds). These also included some big houses. When walking from our grandparents' house to the church, the walk is downhill, ending up at the "bajio" (lower land). The church and the municipal buildings are in the "central" (center) of Rayón.

We drive down into the town and to the back of my grandparents' home. Somehow, the town knows we have arrived. Kids appear from every corner. The older ones, tugging on their shirts while the younger ones are sucking on a candy or wiping their snotty noses. The car is a luxury to them. We are the "Americana" girls. They are curious and so they stare.

Then out comes my nana and tías. Nana's hug is tight, and I'm stuck between her breasts. I can smell the smoke from the wooden stove. I can smell the scent of the Pumada de la Campana cream she rubbed on her skin that morning. Tía Chalita is wearing an apron. She is the chef of the family and that is one of the many things we look forward to. Tata (grandfather) is still out in the fields. We won't see him until the evening.

Right after the greetings, we help Tía Amelia take down our luggage and ice chest filled with deli meats and goodies that were hard to get in Rayón at that time. They especially liked when we took a whole ham.

Once all settled, I go up the hill to greet Tía Chata.

"Ai, la Chinita," Tía Chata exclaims with open arms! She calls me her little Chinese girl, as a term of endearment. As noted earlier, they think we could be part Asian.

Ana Lidia is the oldest child and my best friend, so I look for her amongst her siblings. I greet them too. She has two sisters and three brothers. Ana Lidia and I are tight. We do everything together. Later when the town received running water, they had a shower built. It is outside behind their house. We love playing in it because it is all cement and very cool, especially in the summer. We play with the dolls, but they are not real "Barbies." They are of some cheap brand. Jesus wants to play with us, but we chase him away. The other two boys were too young, and so they left us alone. Ana Lidia's other two sisters were also not interested.

One of the highlights at this younger age, is the daily sale of the "jamoncillos." Tía Chata makes these candies from whole milk, fresh from the cow! She adds tons of sugar and boils the two ingredients and sometimes adds vanilla. She'll test the texture by dropping a big drop onto a plate and passing it to me. She knows I love eating it soft. I also love the burnt pieces. The consistency should be firm but not too hard to be able to form a ball. When done, she lines a basket with a clean kitchen cloth and adds the jamoncillos and covers them with another clean cloth. Ana Lidia and I find a rebozo (long colorful silky shawl) that will shield us from the sun. Ana Lidia holds one end and I hold the other end, so it looks like a canopy. We go door to door selling them.

It's a sunny and very warm day, as most days are in this small Sonoran town! I tighten the grip on my end of the rebozo. We walk the dirt roads, shuffling our feet, leaving dust behind us. As we enter the corridors of those buying our jamoncillos we carelessly leave dust on their newly polished floors.

Most days we sell out immediately, other days it is slow. The money we make is taken back to Tía Chata. Sometimes, she has us stop by a changarro to buy limes. She makes fresh lime juice for lunch. It is sweet and refreshing.

During our route, we at times experience the unexpected.

My brother Stephen with me at a changarro in Rayón.

My First Rayón Funeral Experience

"At sunset the little soul that had come with the dawning went away, leaving heartbreak behind it."
—L.M. Montgomery

On this day, while going door to door selling jamoncillos, we are stopped as we hear wailing coming from a house not too far from where we stood. Along the road, the town folk are whispering about the baby who had died last night. She was merely just eight months old. She had died of some unexpected complication or some incurable disease. There were many rumors flying and at the end I never found out the real cause. When we approached the home, the wailing became louder.

"Out of respect, you need to cry, "Ana Lidia whispers to me. This was going to be hard as I rarely shed tears, nor can I cry on command.

We finally make it to the house and what we find is a small table in the middle of the corridor with the baby lying in a small coffin, dressed in a beautiful, white-laced baptismal gown. It looks

71

like she is simply napping. Her mother soaks a cloth in alcohol and rubs the baby's skin. The bottom of the coffin is kept iced. This was to keep her from smelling and hopefully preserve her until they could bury her. Most of the surrounding Sonoran towns lacked facilities for embalming the body so the burial takes place within 24 hours of the death, if not sooner.

The room is filled with women, faces covered with their rebozos, crying, some just staring at the baby or watching the other women. I am relieved when we are sent outside to join the younger kids. We help ourselves to the refreshments, horchata, tortas (sandwiches) and candy. The homemade horchata is the best. It is rice, whole cinnamon, and water. This mix is soaked overnight. The next day, the cinnamon is removed, and the rest is blended, and sugar and powdered cinnamon are added to one's taste. We forget we are selling jamoncillos!

Farther down closer to the corrals is where we find the men congregated, drinking beer, smoking, and quietly staring into the bonfire, one stirring the burning mesquite. The father of the baby holds his straw hat, looking in the direction of the house where his baby lies.

We stayed for a short time and then left to put the left-over jamoncillos away. We are young and curious and wanted to get back to the baby's house to participate in the funeral activities. The men are carrying the tiny coffin, leading the procession to the church. The women begin to recite the rosary and the children, and the men respond.

After the ceremony, the procession continues to the cemetery. The total walking distance is about one mile, but seems farther because of the steep, sometimes rocky hills. Once at the cemetery, the men finish digging the hole deep enough for the coffin. The coffin is placed in the hole, the priest blesses the baby, and the wailing begins almost as an answer to the prayers.

After the funeral, everyone is invited back to the baby's home and food and drinks are shared. As in the U.S., neighbors bring dishes to share. Later in the evening the women remain and begin a nine-day novena. At this time, the mourning begins by wearing black clothes for a full year and it is very disrespectful to be caught wearing a colored garment. In the past, the black clothes were required by all immediate family members. Today, it is mainly the adults in Mexico who kept the tradition. For example, when my dad passed away, here in the U.S., Mom nor any of the children wore black garments. When Tía Fina's husband passed away in Mexico, she wore black for a year, even when she came to the U.S. to care for Mom. Her daughter, Ana, chose to wear dull colors. It is also expected that the family does not engage in "fun" activities such as going to a dance, movie, or concert for at least three months from the burial, mainly in Mexico. This was my first experience as a child in Mexico. Years later when my grandfather passed away the very same custom was repeated.

Celebrations and Getting Into Trouble

*"Tell me that the purpose of life is to have fun,
and without a care in the world I'll begin wreaking
havoc on everything I pass.
Now that's what I call pure, honest fun."*
—Criss Jami, Killosophy

Birthdays, confirmations, and baptisms are a big deal, especially birthdays. One of my grandparents' neighbor's daughters invited me to her birthday party. Her dad and brothers hung streamers from Nana's house and across the street to their house. They added a rope in the same way to hang a piñata. The festivities began at the birthday girl's home and eventually everyone ended up on the street. The street was blocked to keep vehicles from passing through.

The boys' birthday celebrations are not as big. They will celebrate with a cake shared with the immediate family and their closest friends. The boys will attend the girls' celebrations especially to get their turn to try to break the piñata.

The piñata is broken after each kid takes a turn swinging at it with a decorated stick. If it's a birthday, the piñata will spit out candy. If it's a baptismal or confirmation, it will spit out coins. So, these are the kid parties in Rayón!

I also had friends that lived at the Calle de Arriba! One of our friends' cousins, Elias and his friend, Carlos, took Ana Lidia and me to the river on horseback. One day, we had gone too far, and it was about to storm. Elias took us to their ranch that was not too far to drop off the saddles and was asked if I was okay riding back barebacked. I am also scared to death of lightning and thunder, but what could I say? I needed to get back to Tata's house. Elias got mounted on the horse first and then I was helped on behind him. We took off in a hurry. I clung on to his shirt for dear life and by the time we got home, I had ripped the buttons off his shirt. My tías didn't know about this and I don't know if they ever found out.

What Tía Fina did find out is about the day I wore one of her new shirts. It was white with tiny pink rose buds. We went out with the same guys. This time we went swimming in a cow's trough! We thought nothing of it. We had a blast. When I got to my Nana's, as soon as I walked into the kitchen, Tía Fina saw her shirt.

"What happened, where were you?" We explained, again thinking nothing of it.

"¡Cochinas! ¡Se van a enfermar! ¡Y la blusa se va a quedar desteñida!" This pretty much means that we are pigs and that we will get sick! And her blouse is now discolored. It sounds so much harsher in Spanish!

One evening while having dinner with Tata, Nana, and Tía Fina, I sit quietly after Tía Fina hollered at me to get out of the scorching sun. "You are going to burn and it's about time you get back home!" I had spent the night with my cousin Ana Lidia and spent the morning playing dress-up.

Nana and Tata were seated at the ends of the table and my tía was directly in front of me so she could give me the eye if I dared to try to speak something disrespectful or if I began to fidget.

The food was passed around: beans, sliced crispy cucumbers, and bright red tomatoes. I watched as Tata took a pinch of coarse salt from a small bowl and sprinkled it on his tomatoes. My mouth watered as I eyed the freshly made stack of tortillas. I reached for one but abruptly stopped as Tata gently slapped my hand and began to say grace. It seemed to be a very long prayer. When it ended, I grabbed a tortilla but waited for Nana to serve the perfectly shredded beef.

Finally, I tear a piece of tortilla, spread it with beans and the beef, and rolled it up into a small burrito. Just as I took the first bite, I felt something crawling down my arm. It was a very tiny bug and I brushed it off. Then my neck began to itch, and I scratched it. I ate a couple more burritos, alternating with a mouth full of cucumbers and tomatoes but my mind was on the itching and trying not to scratch. Then my tía whispers something to Nana and they both laughed. I saw Nana's stomach bouncing from the force of the laughter, then Tata laughed, and I joined in but have no idea why until Nana blurted out that I have "piojos" or lice.

After dinner Nana took me out to the corridor and filled a basin with water and washed my hair. We sat on the corridor steps. She sat on the top and I sat on the lower step between her legs so she could easily comb my hair with a lice comb. I imagined hundreds of lice. The more I thought of those little creatures crawling in my hair the more anxious I got but the combing was soothing and so I finally calmed down.

As the story goes today, I didn't have thousands of lice playing in my hair but just one or two and no nits in sight!

Nana Adventures

"Grandmothers are voices of the past and role models of the present. Grandmothers open the doors to the future."
—Helen Ketchum

When I'm being a good granddaughter, I like going to the milpa (field) to take Tata his lunch. Nana makes him a "lonche" (same as lunch). She or my tías make bread or tortillas in the early morning. She fills the bread with beans and meat and tomato slices. She puts the sandwich in a cloth and adds cucumber slices and other vegetables of the day. She folds the cloth over the lonche. She then takes another cloth, puts the wrapped lonche on it and brings the four corners together. Nana ties a knot and puts a long stick through the knot to carry it with. She'll take empty gunny sacks. We walk side by side to the field. I don't speak a lot of Spanish, so we walk quietly. Nana loves laughing at my Spanish. One day she was yelling at me to bring her the "palangana." I ignored her. I didn't think she was speaking to me until she shouts, "Silvia, traeme la palangana!" I tell her I don't know what she wants. She laughed for days and told the story to everyone who walked into their house. The palangana is a basin made of metal. She used a big one to soak white clothes. She had another one in the kitchen that she'd use for strained milk and the one she washed my hair in.

We get to Tata's field. He is sitting by the well, shoes off and his pants rolled up. He has a big smile when he sees me. We stay with him while he eats and then we clean up and fill the gunny sacks with green chilies or onions. It could also be tomatoes or garlic or whatever is in harvest.

We return home; Nana, with the sacks over her back, gets the look from the town folk. It's a man's job, not for a woman!" My grandmother ignores them.

At about 2:30 Tata returns home and has hot coffee, even in the heat of the summer. They say it is cooling. He has a cochito with it. The best way to describe it is like a gingerbread cookie but shaped into a pig. A cochito is a piglet. When I eat gingerbread cookies, I am taken back to these days. The lady that lived across from Nana's made most of the cochitos. They traded off veggies for the cochito.

Other times, Nana took me to pick ripe "pitayas" (prickly pear). The skin is tough red with sharp needles. The inside is red with black seeds. It is very sweet but hard to clean. There is another fruit picked that is about one or two inches in length, green on the outside and inside with seeds and we call it "tuna." Some argue that the tuna is the prickly pear.

When going to pick the pitayas, we wear long-sleeved shirts and covered our heads with a rebozo. I carried an empty metal pail and Nana carried a long stick with a metal fork that was homemade. It is like what we use in the states called a fruit picker but not as fancy. We used it for reaching the prickly pears that were up high. We walked through the streets until we get to the base of the mountain. By then, we have a group of kids following us. All was fun and Nana enjoyed it as well.

Sometimes I think I could have been an archaeologist. I always looked for odd things hidden in the ground or in between bushes. Tío Vayo, Tía Tili's husband, took us to his field one late afternoon. His fields are very large. I never knew where his land started and where it ended. As I was walking through the brush, I saw something shining. It was a piece of a pot. It had a blue flower design, and the background was white. This was unusual that a pretty pot had landed in this field. A little further down, I find another piece. I picked each piece and showed them to my tío. He told us a story of the Yaqui Indians who lived on his land many years ago. He said that when he's there late in the day, he sees spirits floating through the brush. He said that we should go one evening with him and we could do some digging to see if we find more artifacts and possibly a ghost. I was thrilled, but unfortunately, we never made it.

He and Tía Tili also owned a ranch. It was about 30 minutes from my grandparents' house. We went a few times to cut figs and one time slept overnight. They had two gigantic trees full of figs. We filled buckets of figs that were later cooked and made into jam. Empanadas were stuffed with the jam and what wasn't cooked we ate.

Tata taking a break to visit with a family friend from the U.S.
He loved to show off his well.

Sylvia (right) with Gloria (middle), and Ana's friend
sitting on top of Tata's well.

Abuelito's house – The back of the corridor in the background with Nana and her great-great grandchildren. Looks like she just made the dough for tortillas.

Abuelitos' (Grandparents) House

"I loved their home. Everything smelled older, worn but safe; the food aroma had baked itself into the furniture."
—Susan Strasberg

Our grandparent's house was the coolest. It is long shaped. It has a long corridor with big round wooden beams holding up the roof. Walking in from the front door, you step into the first bedroom. This room has a cabinet that keeps Tata's mezcal. Across from the front door is the kitchen separating the bedroom with a cloth curtain. From the kitchen there is a door leading to the corridor. The kitchen also has a large window that opens to a road rarely used, other than when the cows that are herded to the pastures. The road separates the house from our Tía Tili's house. Her house also has the large window facing the road. They can visit without having to leave the house. The aromas from their kitchens intertwines, making the stomachs crave for a little bite from each kitchen! Tía Tili was the soda lady. Once they had electricity, she filled her refrigerator with sodas. Neighbors and the Americana's liked going over to buy their favorite, La Fanta, the orange-flavored soda.

In the first bedroom, there is another door leading to the second bedroom. Then from this bedroom there is a small hallway. The hallway to the right takes you to the street. If you go the left, it takes you to the back corridor. Across from the second bedroom and across from the hallway is another room.

This room has a red velvet love seat on one side and in the other side there are two matching chairs. There is a coffee table. I thought this would be a formal living room, but it's where my tías met with their future husbands. There was always a chaperone sitting on the other end in one of the chairs.

Across from this room there are double doors. They lead to a big closet that doubles as a storage room. There were two big trunks that I liked rummaging through. They contained old stuff. Some held Tío Manual's leather whips, blankets and bridles once used on his horses. My tías' clothes were hanging all along this room. There is another door on the left side that leads to another bedroom. This bedroom belonged to my Tata's sister. She was known as Trini! She was old and mean. We used to take her dinner and wondered why she didn't walk to the kitchen if it was only steps away. My cousin told me stories of ghosts living there. I stayed away from this room.

The second room was my favorite. It had a dresser and a big armoire that was always locked up. When my tías unlocked it, I discovered pretty things like mantillas that my nana and tías wore to mass. They were made from lace or were crocheted with beautiful silky thread. They covered their heads before entering the church. They had a box with pretty hair combs and other treasures. Not expensive, but pretty. There was also a queen bed. It was originally my grandparents' then it became the daughters. Most of the family slept on cots outside in the corridor. I slept with my cousin, Ana Lidia's younger sister Cecilia. She practically lived with my grandparents. She ran errands for them and helped with chores.

During the day we all took siestas. To get away from the flies, I slept under the bed on top of a "petate." The petate is a grass mat. It was also the coolest place. No one had me sleeping there and Nana tried to scare me that I could get stung by a scorpion, but I didn't care.

I also sleepwalked. Tía Fina had to bring me back into the room a few times. One time, she caught me petting their dog outside on the front pavement. Another time, she caught me wiping my feet and putting my shoes on; and then she allowed me outside. We slept with doors and windows open. There was no fear of invasions or thefts at night nor in the day. There were some drunks, but Nana welcomed them into her kitchen. She fed them. Most drunks were relatives of relatives.

This same room is where Tía Chalita gave birth to her oldest son. When she gave the sign that she was ready to deliver, a midwife was called, and I was put out in the corridor with a basket of clothes to iron. My grandmother and my tías helped by boiling water and gathering towels. As I ironed my Tata's long underwear, I could hear my tía screaming in agony and then silence and then the baby's cry! Nana always laughed that I, the Americana, ironed Tata's underwear! But they never said anything about me witnessing the commotion, screams, and finally the birth. Makes me chuckle, too.

The town didn't stay safe. Years later, my nana and Tía Chalita had a terrible experience, as I was told. One day, a group of Judicial Police (corrupted police), stormed into my grandparents' home. My grandfather had already passed away. Tía Chalita and her husband, Tony, lived there to care for Nana. The police were looking for marijuana plants. Someone had tipped them off that my uncle had plants growing somewhere. The police bound my nana and Tía Chalita to the corridor chairs as they rummaged through their house. They tore into the bed mattresses and took everything out of drawers. Tia Chalita and Tony still don't understand what they were looking for in the house. They took my uncle with them and interrogated him. He was burned with cigarettes and was brutally hit until they finally believed that he didn't have marijuana plants. This was a very sad time.

Church and Night Sights

"But I do believe in the paranormal, that there are things our brains just can't understand.
—Art Bell

Father Sandoval, the priest who married my parents, was still the pastor, now much older and crankier. When we went to mass on Sunday, my tías made us wear a round lace on the top of our head, held with bobby pins. We were not allowed to wear sleeveless clothes and we couldn't wear pants. Dresses had to be below the knee.

"Aqui vienen las Americanas! Here come the American girls!" Fr. Sandoval would say when he saw us walking into church. There were a few times when I wore a sleeveless dress, so I had to wear a long mantilla that fell over my shoulders and pray he didn't notice. One time I wore pants. He came by and hit my knee with his cane but didn't make me leave.

The church was split. The altar faces a set of pews and on the left side there is another set of pews. That side of the church was for the men. The other for the women. This went on for many years. When the Americanas went to church, the boys and girls sat on the men's side and that would really irritate Fr. Sandoval. Eventually, the rules changed, and men mixed with women on either side. Interestingly, more men started to join their wives, especially men that didn't want to attend before. The dress code was also more relaxed.

It was also known that the church and Tía Fina's house are built on an old cemetery. Women have recounted stories of ghosts appearing while the women were praying alone. When we stay at Tía Fina's house, I'm always leery of a ghost hiding under the bed, or floating in the damp, cold air. I keep my feet tucked under the sheets!

Speaking of ghosts. Once when I slept at my cousin's house, we stayed up late one night looking at the stars. Rayón did not have electricity until years later and when the village did, it was restricted for a short period at night. The nights were beautiful. The stars were super bright. This one night we were looking toward one of the mountains when suddenly a "bulto" of fire (ball of fire) came rolling down the mountain. We didn't know what it was then, but later determined it was a meteorite.

Another time we saw the Milky Way. It filled the sky. Thousands of stars formed into a big sea lion with a long tail. That's the best I could describe it. The cluster of stars made for beautiful shades of color. I was so blessed to have witnessed these two gifts from our Creator!

On the nights without electricity, when at Nana's home the women and kids sat outside on the sidewalks. We lit kerosene lamps if we stayed out beyond dusk. When it rained, the toads came out. Cecilia and I chased them and sprinkled salt on their backs to see them swell. Nana caught us doing this once and made us go inside, telling us that the toads will jump on our beds and choke us while sleeping. That was kind of cruel of her, but we were cruel to the poor toads and deserved being scared for one night! We never hurt a toad after that.

The Shower

Kerosene got me in trouble. It was in later years when Rayón finally got hooked up for electricity. It was for certain hours of the night, but we also enjoyed it through the day. At that time, restrooms and showers were built attached to the houses. Nana's house had one attached to the kitchen, but the entrance was on the outside facing the flower garden. The bathroom had a connecting room that was used by our Tío Manuel. The room contained his saddles and ropes and what else he needed for his horses. There was also hay that he brought in on his boots or from the saddles being dragged in from the corrals. I loved the smell of hay. It was probably the horse and cow manure I was smelling and didn't know the difference.

I was excited to shower in a real shower but there was one thing I didn't know. There was no hot water. To receive hot water, we had to warm the pipes. There is a small nook outside on the shower wall that houses a pipe and a burner. I didn't know there was a special oil used to light it. I used the kerosene and was quite surprised when it blew up. I jumped back and escaped getting burned. This is exactly what Mom did when she was younger, but it was when she spilled it on burning wood.

The shower worked fine but it was the darkness that got to me. I hate spiders and in Rayón there were many daddy long-legs. Because the bathroom lighting was so dim, it was darker in the shower. When I took showers, I went in and out as fast as I could. I didn't want to see a spider, nor did I want them crawling on my feet.

A couple days before we had to leave to go back to Tucson, I allowed my cousin to pierce my ears. We hid this from my tía. We took two cubes of ice and put one over each side of my ear lobe. When it was numb enough, she burned the tip of a sewing needle and forced it into the lobe. When my tías found out, they were livid. Mom was even angrier when one of them got infected a few days after we returned home.

When our stay in Rayón ended, we said our good-byes to everyone. More hugs and crying. Nana and our tías sent us home with tortillas and jamoncillos and other sweets. Nana stuffed our suitcases with her crocheted beautiful doilies in many sizes and shapes. Even today, I have one big one on a corner table in our dining room and another one that looks more like a blanket that is draped over an old church pew in our bedroom. They were made and given with so much love that I hope one day my own daughter or nieces will appreciate them.

Entering and Exiting Eighth Grade

Back in Tucson, I was now entering the eighth grade. We were preparing to graduate and enter high school. Mom and Dad decided to enroll us at Salpointe Catholic High School. Most of our friends went to public schools. Our neighbors went to Pueblo High School, right behind St. John the Evangelist school and church. I wanted to join my friends, but our parents insisted on the Catholic schools.

It was a fun year. We had been grouped into teams to plan our graduation night. I was selected to be the artist of the graduation program. I loved to paint and draw so I was happy they chose me. I was also relieved as I wasn't confident enough to think I could come up with songs that I didn't know or words of wisdom to add to the program. I chose to draw zodiac signs with lots of color but not too crazy. It was approved and was used. I was so proud of it when I saw it printed and saw parents holding it in their hands at graduation.

Rayón As Teenagers

Another summer and I knew it was close to being one of my last two long summers in Rayón. Our hormones were changing, we started looking at boys. Both Ana Lidia and I already had some in mind. Ana my sister, went just for the long weekend and returned with Tía Amelia. She was older so she already had guys serenading her.

There was a guy who was short, goofy-looking and always drunk so we told Ana he was serenading her next. She hated us teasing her about him and felt worse when he'd ask her to dance. She knew we were watching as she refused to dance with him. He finally left her alone.

After she left it was just me hanging out with Ana Lidia and Mom's cousin Chalita. Chalita moved to Tucson when Laurie had her first child. She never married so she has taken care of all of Laurie's children and most of my siblings' kids and now their kids. She also makes us great mini empanadas and roasted peanuts for our parties.

We liked being around Chalita because she was much older and had accumulated many friends, male and female. So, she knew which cowboy had a truck we could jump on and ride around town with. The trucks were used for hauling hay, so they all had racks. Some were removable and so those were the trucks we liked getting into. Sometimes there would be five or more girls standing if it had rails or sitting if it didn't. We sang all through the town. My tías got wind that I was one of the girls, so they immediately asked me to never do that again! But did I listen?

Día de San Juan is the feast day of St. John the Baptist. He is the patron saint of rain. When there is no rain and fear of a drought, the people pray that on this day the rain will come. The feast day is important to the people of Rayón and so the town takes advantage of the day with a full-blown celebration. There are dances after horse races. The streets are decorated with banners made from tissue, just like the birthday party banners. Those that are to race, show their racehorses throughout the day, riding under the banners. The festivities and the races are held at the aterrizaje. This is an area a few miles past the cemetery at the end of town. The land was later used for landing small planes. Even some of the Malloy family flew their private single engine prop plane to meet Tía Amelia's family and landed on this field.

Booths were set up to sell burritos and tacos. Another was for sweets, including paletas, raspados, and granisados. The granisado is a raspado served in a cup, with a scoop of homemade vanilla ice-cream on the bottom. Then the ice followed by flavored syrup. My favorite was the homemade vanilla paleta. Paleta is like a Popsicle.

Since Ana Lidia and I were not 15, we were not allowed to go to the dance unless we were accompanied by our tías. We didn't mind, so we went and had fun watching all the couples dance and watching men get turned down.

At some point during this trip, my cousin and I ended up with a boyfriend. It started outside of Ana Lidia's house. Ana Lidia's mom watched us through her kitchen window. Then slowly we became gutsy and started meeting our boy friends at the cemetery to have raspados from a nearby changarro. We sat on the cemetery's cement wall to visit, as everyone else did. Then we got even more gutsy and decided to go to the movies. The movie theatre was in the back of someone's home. The entrance was someone at the door taking your money and letting you go through. To get to the theatre we took the short cut, through a dry arroyo (wash). Ana Lidia slowed down behind us and so when we turned around to see how far back Ana Lidia and her boyfriend were, we see them kissing! We weren't going to be left behind, so my boyfriend and I walked back to where they were when suddenly, Tía Amelia is screaming for us to go home from a great tía's porch who lived right next to the arroyo. I was more alarmed because I didn't know Tía Amelia was back in town. That was the end of that summer.

An example of people (mainly girls) getting into the bed of the trucks
and a cowboy driving them around town.
This is a more current picture. We were trying to recreate the old times.

Bud and Amelia when they first met.

Bud and Amelia in later years.

Uncle Bud

"We do not need to know the beginning of a child's story to change the ending."
—Fi Newood

Tía Amelia married Uncle Bud. He came into our lives for a reason. He owned a foreign car-part garage in town and had land far out west of Tucson where he kept junk cars to use for parts. He had a few employees. He also fostered children and at that time he was still fostering one young man who worked for him. He originally came from Iowa and still owned farmland there.

Uncle Bud took us on rides in his dune buggy and taught Laurie and me how to drive a motorcycle. We crashed into a mesquite tree and never rode it again! We weren't badly hurt but it was enough to scare us.

When Uncle Bud witnessed some of Dad's moods, he had a man-to-man talk with him. He also noticed that the boys didn't have much to do around the house. So, he asked Dad for permission to take them to work with him. Not for child labor but just to teach them mechanics and mainly to keep them out of trouble. He also favored me. He probably felt sorry for me. He took me to his shop in the summers, and on some weekends. I went with him for two or three days of the week. I alphabetized his receipts and invoices, and cleaned bolts or whatever else he gave me. This is where we drank soda behind Mom's back. The boys loved it when he'd give them a quarter to choose their favorite soda. We went home smelling like grease. The boys dressed in their oldest clothes, sometimes mismatched.

After a while, I stopped working with him and stayed home helping Mom. Shortly before I stopped going to the shop, I bought a new pair of grownup eyeglasses. Uncle Bud noticed and told me he loved how they looked! It made me happy and this time, I was excited to show them off at school!

Uncle Bud took our CYO (Christian Youth Organization) group to the Chiricahua Mountains for a weekend retreat. Since he had a truck with an extended back, with racks, many of us fit and so did all our supplies. He loved doing things for us.

The CYO was for young adults, beginning with high school. We had meetings and worked at fundraisers for the church. We also participated in a retreat; once a year, all CYO groups from the Diocese gathered in one large venue for a dance.

When I was in college, Uncle Bud took me to Hermosillo to translate. He was either selling car parts or was looking to buy a unique car part. The parts were for stocking in his foreign car part shop, Tasler Motors. I didn't enjoy doing this because I didn't know how to translate car parts into Spanish. I didn't even know what they were in English! I went because it made him and Tía Amelia happy!

Rehearsal before queen festivities with Virginia, the runner up.

**Day of queen event held during summer festivities.
The young man is David, a friend.**

Last Summer in Rayón – Queen

*"People are like music: some speak the truth
and others are just noise."*
—Unknown

The summer after my freshman year, I went to Rayón to stay for a couple of weeks, and it became the last long summer. By then, I was teased that I had one foot in Mexico and one in the U. S.! My speech became a problem. I didn't know Spanish very well, and my English wasn't good, either! The cousins and their friends called me "mocha!" It was an insult. It's a slang word meaning I was dumb because I couldn't speak either language. How did they know I couldn't speak English if they didn't know a drop of it? They were just mean. Even the women told us how fat or skinny we are. Once, Chalita's mom greeted me with "ay que gordita," meaning I was chubby. One of her sons who walked in at that moment scolded her and told her I looked healthy, not fat!

On this trip, I was chosen to be queen. It was a tradition to select a queen for the summer festivities and the queen was selected from the out-of-town females. Today, they select a town queen for the chance to move on to the State pageants, like in the U.S., Miss America. I got this honor, although, it wasn't for anything special I did, nor was it a vote. They put all the out-of-town names in a bowl; someone chooses one and reads off the name. Not liking attention, I first refused it but was talked into going with the process. This was part of the festivities that included horse races. The dance for this occasion was held at the "placita," a plaza in the middle of town, with a gazebo right in the middle.

I didn't have a long dress, so I spent a couple of days with Ana Luisa, one of my new friends, trying on her dresses. She was a little taller than me but same weight. I tried on a few of her dresses and settled for a tangerine-colored one. It had spaghetti straps. I was a little worried about wearing it because the older ladies criticized young girls for wearing immodest clothes. The dress needed to be altered because it was too long!

On the day of the festivities, we drove around in the back of Ana Luisa's brother's truck waving to people standing in front of their homes. They were waving at the Queen! Oh my! At least I was in my regular clothes, and it wasn't obvious as to who the real queen was.

Finally, the evening came. Ana Luisa helped me with my hair, and I borrowed some make up. I thought I looked nice! She explains what will happen at night when I am introduced. There is also a runner-up, and she will join me. Her name is Virginia.

We walk up the stairs of the gazebo to get into the enclosed area. They announced Virginia and me. We walked around waving at the audience, the band is playing in the distance. People are clapping and yelling, then I heard a man's voice shouting, "Que fea la reina! ¡Toda flaca!" "What an ugly queen! Too skinny!" It hit me like as if he had thrown a rock at me. I kept my composure, but felt a little better when David, a friend of mine, yelled back at him to look at himself in the mirror!

The hurt didn't last long because the dance music began, and we enjoyed every bit of it. My tías allowed me to dance with relatives. There was one older second cousin who always found his way over to me to take me to the dance floor. He had green eyes and light brown hair. He could have been handsome, but he was always drunk. His face looked much older when he drank. My tías knew that when he took me out to dance, they had to prepare to pry him away from me. He got very close to me so couples dancing next to me also put their arms between us and gave him a look, warning him to stay back. After a few of these incidents, I hid when I saw him coming my way.

We learned to dance cumbias and corridos with our uncles and distant cousins or just with the girls. The best part was when a few couples began the train dance. They hang on to the waist of the person in front and dance around the dance floor, picking up more dancers until the dance floor is nothing but the train. It goes on until the song ends.

In future years, these were the dances we most enjoyed. We tried going on the days of holidays because those were the most entertaining times for both parents and the teenage girls!

My sister Ana went with me on this last long trip. Right before it was time to return home, she received a letter from Laurie. Laurie wrote that Dad bought a new car. Ana got excited and couldn't wait to get home. When we arrive, she's looking for the car but there is no new car! Laurie had lied. It was mean but we laughed anyway! We did find furniture moved around and new bunkbeds for the boys. This meant that Ana, Laurie, and I no longer had to share two beds pushed together.

High School New Experiences

"The prettiest smile hides the deepest secrets.
The prettiest eyes have cried the most tears.
And the kindest hearts have felt the most pain."
—Unknown

I was starting high school, a Catholic one! Then came the kid pranks, called bullying today. I also found out that I was not American enough.

I was put in special reading and math classes, adding to further humiliation — only to find out that it was to my advantage.

These were the years to worry about the big things like proms and winter formals and quinceañeras and knowing it was time to decide future education. I struggle finding transportation until I learned to drive at 19 years of age.

Summers were spent, finding ways to keep me from boredom. At home there cannot be boredom, or something worse than boredom was assigned. My artistic talent was revealed but disappointing when it turned out not to be affordable.

Painful physical changes began when Rheumatoid Arthritis struck. Then on top of the pain, I began looking for work and finding myself in a new world, some good and some bad — and keeping a secret.

High School

*"I'm not telling you it's going to be easy —
I'm telling you it's going to be worth it."*
— Art Williams

Going to high school was a game changer. We were driven away from our home to get educated but it was also the beginning of detaching from the only environment we knew.

I would soon learn a new routine, new rules, and more humiliation.

I was on my way to meet new people and new teachers.

There would be new lessons and new disappointments.

The summers were for finding my talent and learning it was not affordable.

I learned that our parents kept us from doing things we thought were important, but it was only because they didn't understand but I didn't know that until much later.

I was excited not to wear a uniform, but the rules were the same as at St. John's, like no short dresses. We could wear pants but no shorts. We had to take the bus. Salpointe was a little over eight miles from our home. We picked up the bus at the corner of the last street in our subdivision. When our friends heard that we were going to Salpointe, they told us that we thought we were better than them. I felt bad because that was not the case. It was just what our parents planned for us.

On my first day, I came home to our new baby brother, Stephen, also the last of six.

High school was a big thing for me, and I was excited to go home and tell everyone what a great day I had and tell them every detail. When I went into the house, everyone was hovering over Stephen! The attention went to him so my first day was just another day!

The first week of my freshman year was learning the class assignments and learning how to use our lockers. I met up with people from grade school, but they weren't my friends. Richard was my only friend, but he was off meeting new ones.

When I finally connected with the girlfriends that lasted, we planned what to wear to school, sometimes colors or a day in identical shirts. Other kids thought we were silly. We didn't care.

Mom made all our clothes, but Annie and Rose's parents occasionally brought us their hand-me-downs. They bought the current style and gave us their old clothes. To us they were like new and the only clothes that were not sewn by Mom, until we went to work. We didn't care and so my sisters and I fought to see who got into the box first.

When we bought something new, it was always just one article to go with one of the hand-me-down pants or to update one of the skirts or pants that Mom made us.

In one of the hand-me-downs, there was a skort. I always wanted to wear one. It is a skirt with attached shorts. I wore it to school and forgot all about it. I had to go to the restroom during one of my classes. I had to go badly so I quickly took the skirt down but forgot to take my underwear down and peed right on them. I didn't know what to do, so I finally took them off and threw them in the garbage. What else would I do with a wet pair of underwear!

I don't recall much more about my freshman year other than that I was having problems keeping up in math and reading.

It was time for cheerleading tryouts for the sophomore year. I wanted to try out badly but didn't know how I would get to the games. There was a set of twins who offered to pick me up, but I thought it would be silly since they lived on the other side of town. They still encouraged me to try out. I prepared, and on weekends a friend trying out who lived a little bit closer to me invited me to ride with her.

The weekend before the tryouts, Dad decides they are going to Rayón. I begged them to let me stay at my friend's house so that I didn't miss tryouts. It didn't happen. I grudgingly packed my bags and went to Rayón. Mom had not seen her family in a while, so Dad decides on this weekend to take them. Why didn't they postpone it for another weekend? No, they did it on the most important weekend of my high school life. My parents didn't understand what it meant to me. I could understand not being able to provide but being in cheerleading wasn't going to cost them anything. Wrong! It did cost money, as I saw my friends having to pay for their uniforms and having to take turns taking treats to share. My parents must have known it would become costly and my dad knew he wasn't going to be driving me back and forth!

Interestingly, Mom ended up making the cheerleaders' uniforms. I don't recall if it was for Salpointe or one of the other schools but every time I saw the uniforms, they brought back memories and the desire to wear one.

It was either late in my freshman year or the beginning of my sophomore year that I was moved to special lessons. A few of us were pulled out of the regular class and taken to another room to be taught math and then a different period to a separate room to be taught special reading. It was in my senior year that I was freed from all the special classes.

I believe that if my parents had sat with me to discuss the reason for the special classes, I would have understood, and it would not have been as bad as I made it out to be. Our parents didn't have meetings with us. They didn't help us sort out our anger nor our misunderstandings.

So, I didn't appreciate the special lessons until I went to Pima College and saw how well I was doing. I did especially well in the Writing classes and enjoyed Sociology and Spanish Literature. I still struggled with math and always will!

During my sophomore year, two bus incidents occurred. My parents were late with the bus fee so as punishment, I was asked to sweep the bus before the rest of the students were allowed in. I swept it while they watched. When I got home, Mom knew something was wrong. I told her about the incident first, and then she told Dad. Dad gets angry and accuses Mom for not paying and then it just gets crazy, and I wished I had not said anything. The bus fees were always paid on time going forward.

The second incident was after school. I had worn one of Ana's dresses. It was made of a light jersey. It was purple with yellow flowers. I liked how the skirt was wide and hung neatly from my small waist. I was on the bus, sitting in the back with my friends. When we got to my stop, there are fewer students on the bus, but all are boys. As I'm walking down the aisle, I hear a chant, "Mooner, mooner!" and laughter. I didn't know it was about me until I got to the front and realized the dress had gone static and was stuck up above my behind. They saw my undies and I was very embarrassed. I got home and threw the dress away. Ana asked why I had thrown her dress away and I explained. I don't recall if she ever wore that dress but if anything, I probably ripped it up to make Barbie clothes. Oh, wait not "Barbie." We had Midge and Tammy.

We had a social room at Salpointe. Students could sit and read or watch TV during breaks. It was the social hour. One time, while sitting on a recliner, Lucas, another neighbor friend, decided to wrap me in masking tape. He came so quickly that I couldn't react. He was laughing as he went around me with the tape. Others stood and watched but didn't stop him. Gloria, my friend wasn't there yet so I was left to fend for myself. I don't recall how I got out of that mess! I was so mad and humiliated. I didn't talk to Lucas for days.

When we were younger, we rarely played at Lucas' house, but when we did, the memory is that his mom gave each of us a packet of sugared Kool-Aid and a Popsicle stick. We licked the stick's end so that the Kool-Aid stuck to it and that's how we ate it. If we didn't get the stick, we poured it on the palm of our hands and used our finger. We went home with a red or purple tongue depending on the flavor. Mom never said anything after the first time, when we had to explain the color of our tongue.

I met Gloria in our Choir class. Neither one of us could sing. The nun had us move our lips after she gave up trying to get us to sing a decent tune. We got bored, so we played the staring game. We stared at each other to see who blinked first. We wore Capezio shoes. They were popular flat dancing shoes with strings tied into bows. We undid the bows and retied them, making it a contest as well. After class we walked out laughing and since then we have been friends.

Gloria and our other two friends went to proms and winter formals together. We didn't have boy dates, at least this one year! At the end of the night of a winter formal, we sat outside to talk to friends. We sat on the lawn that was facing the main street so that we could watch the couples leaving the party and we gossiped. We wore long formal dresses. After our friends left, we stayed until the sprinklers scared us away. We were soaked by the time we walked out onto the parking lot. I snuck into my house but when Mom was looking for something in the room, she saw the dress and the stains the water left. At first, she thought we had been drinking but was fine when I told her the story.

Gloria is the one who drove me around and the only reason why I could attend some of the school functions. She picked me up to go to football games. She also took us to the drive-in. One of those nights we took my sister, Laurie. None of us were at a drinking age but we had beer with us. Laurie drank one bottle and that was enough for her. She was laughing at everything. We went to the restroom and made sure she looked sober in case we saw someone our parents knew. Laurie went into the stall. When she came out, I heard her greeting Mrs. Altamirano, a neighbor and good friend of Mom's. I called Laurie over and waved to Mrs. Altamirano! The next challenge was getting Laurie into our house without her bumping into the walls. We made it but still wonder if Mom or Dad suspected anything but kept quiet.

The summer after my junior year was somewhat boring. Not going to Rayón, I had to find something to entertain myself. I had found a magazine that was advertising art classes. There were two drawings in pencil. One was a dog and the other a woman. I chose the dog. I sketched it and it was pretty good! I mailed it without telling my parents. A few weeks later, Dad gets a call from a salesman. The man tells Dad that they thought I had potential and would like to visit to discuss a plan. Dad didn't know what to expect so he invited him over. A week later a man with a big black briefcase appeared. We sat in the dining room. The man pulled out a portfolio of many drawings.

"She really does have potential." He tried to convince Dad to enroll me in the school.

Dad said he would think about it. He is given a couple of days to decide. When the time came to give the salesman an answer, Dad became nervous and on edge. He finally picked up the phone and told him he couldn't afford it and hung up. He looked at me with sad eyes. "I'm sorry but we can't do it right now!" he said.

I didn't want to make it worse, so I brushed it off like it was no big deal. It reminded me of how I felt when I was in grade school and wanted to keep a rented flute, but they couldn't afford to buy a new one nor a used one.

I think this is why we give Melissa, our daughter, so much more. We over-did it on Christmas and on her birthday. When she was older, she wanted to learn modeling, so we took her to modeling classes during the summer and on weekends when school was in session. She auditioned and made it but was too shy or who knows why; she decided to stop going. She learned how to apply makeup and how to walk gracefully. She was not deprived of anything. Thank God we only had one child!

In my senior year, I took shorthand. I didn't do very well. The teacher pulled me aside one day as I was walking out of the classroom to try to encourage me to continue taking it in college. She thought I was doing well enough and just needed more practice. She ended up in the hospital and so Gloria and I went to visit her. While talking, she told me, "I know why you weren't doing well with shorthand. You were too busy asking for the hall pass, to flirt with Bob." That totally caught me off guard, but I laughed because I knew it was true!

Bob was a little taller than I, with lots of curly hair. It appeared like he always wore white pants. He talked to me, just in passing. He was also Gloria's neighbor.

One time when I was at Gloria's for a party, it must have been a family party. Bob was there and since we didn't know many of the guests, we sat alone on a bench in the backyard. We talked about school and our future. At one point, he leaned over and whispered, "You know, you are not American enough for me!" I was crushed, yet I didn't move, and we kept talking as if nothing had been said.

Twenty years later at our 20th class reunion, Bob was there, talking with another guy. I took my husband over to introduce him to Bob. I told Bob the story of him breaking my heart! He said, "Where have you been all my life?" Followed by, "Did I say that?"

"You must have been high on pot!" his friend told him as he pounded on his chest.

We all laughed! He told me he married a Chinese lady but then divorced. I almost said that she wasn't American enough either.

At the end of our senior year, I was still worried about what to study in college. Most of my friends knew their destination. My graduation was not a big deal. The only exciting day was the last swimming/yearbook party! It was also the day that Richard realized that I had grown up! I wore a white two-piece bathing suit that Dad scolded me for buying and then Mom for allowing it, yet she had nothing to do with it. I still wore it. At one point Richard came to me and said very protectively, "Why are you wearing that? You are showing everything! Cover yourself with the towel!" I just shrugged and walked away! We played games and ate hamburgers while we had our classmates sign our yearbooks.

High school graduation picture - 1974.

Summer After High School – New Beginnings

"She was powerful, not because she wasn't scared but because she went on so strongly despite the fear."
— Atticus

There was so much anticipation looking forward to going to college but to afford it, I had to work. I didn't receive scholarships, and my parents were not going to provide. I either found work to pay for school, or I didn't go.

In the meantime, Ana was already attending the University of Arizona, Laurie was a couple of grades behind me in high school and soon going to college. I found that I was left in the middle doing nothing and I was not going to stand for that. I was not going to stay behind.

Here are my first experiences at my simple positions but they served a purpose: One, to teach me customer service; second, how to fend off sexual harassment; and third, to keep my head up high even when at its worst.

I also learned to never stay at a position I didn't like because that would not be good for the company, the customer, or myself.

The first real job was through a friend. Colette had a brother managing at a Kentucky Fried Chicken franchise on Sixth Avenue, south Tucson. It was a block farther from our grade school but not so far that I couldn't walk if I didn't find a ride. I thought it was good enough for starters, so Colette asked her brother, James, to interview me. He was the manager. He hired me on the spot. There was a manager assistant, Vincent. It was just him, James, and me. I was taught how to use the cash register. It was the old clunky one, not computerized. I learned how to ring up the order, how to clean the eating area and the outside bathrooms. We were to take turns cleaning the bathrooms.

There were problems with the customers. We had drunk and dirty old men coming in. One Mexican man told me he wanted two pints of milk and pointed at my top and laughed. I pressed the alert button that was underneath the counter and James immediately came up front and asked him to leave. A second time, a man came in to order multiple family orders. After I rang him up, he told me he needed separate receipts. I didn't know how to separate the receipts and the register was not flexible, so I was stuck. He then raised his voice at me with customers standing in line behind him. "Didn't you go to school? Can't you figure it out? You are so dumb! You need to go back to school!"

He was so angry and kept getting closer to me. I thought he was going to punch me out, so I pressed the button and James immediately came up and tried calming him. He told him it was his mistake for not requesting separate receipts when he placed the order and asked him to leave. The man paid, and took his change out of James hand, and grabbed his bags and left!

These were very small issues compared to what came next. It was my turn to clean the outside bathroom. It was early in the evening and James had already gone home. When I went into the bathroom and was cleaning the sink with my back to the door, Vincent walked in and started groping me. I fought him until he knew he wouldn't get to me and left. I quickly locked the door. He had grabbed my blouse at one point, so my buttons were undone. I was shaking so hard that I couldn't button it fast enough. I waited before leaving. I still felt frightened that he might be outside waiting.

I left him to close the restaurant and I went home without telling him. I shook and cried all the way home but stopped a few minutes before to get rid of any signs I had been crying. I couldn't tell my parents. I was afraid they would blame me or wouldn't believe me. I didn't tell anyone for many, many years. The next day, I went in, only to tell James I was quitting. He couldn't understand why but I was too ashamed to tell him. I lied to my parents. I told them they didn't need me.

It wasn't until much later I realized that I should have said something then. Who knows how many others this guy molested without anyone reporting him, just like me? And because of this, I hate going into public restrooms. If I absolutely need to use one, I get in and out as quickly as I can.

I needed to find something else to do, so I applied at different places. In the meantime, I applied for a Children's Literature Writing class. They allowed me to make monthly payments. I had saved enough for the first month. The way it worked is that a professor was assigned to me. She sent me a book with instructions and tear-outs. I was to complete the first assignment, mail it back to her and then she returned it with comments and a grade. I did this for about a year. I went through all the assignments and even entered some of her approved stories to publishers but never had one accepted.

While I continued corresponding with the Writing class, Mom found me work with a friend's husband. He picked me up early in the morning and brought me home at the end of the day. I worked at his print shop, printing, and collating documents. It was very uncomfortable driving with him, but he turned out to be a nice man and very respectable.

I then received a call from a furniture store. I stopped working at the print shop to work at the furniture store. The office manager and I sat in the same office. It was small and she was a screamer. If she didn't like something I did, she would angrily show me the right way. She was also mean to the warehouse guy, John. John and I had lunch together. We also went for walks around the site. Our hands would touch, and I didn't think anything about it. We became close "friends!" We shared our frustrations about this woman. She might have been the owner's wife. We finely parted ways when I left to start the first college semester and he left to go to the Navy.

I didn't remember John until 40 years later when my husband was going through boxes in the garage. There was a manila folder labeled "Personal" and my name was next to it. I opened it and found an old wallet and some old letters. In the wallet were two pictures of John, one in citizen clothes and one in uniform. The uniform picture had writing on the back. It said that he didn't want to send me a picture of himself but because I had asked, he thought to send the one in uniform. Then he says he's coming back for Christmas and would like to see me. I don't know what happened to John. I don't know if he tried calling me, and I ignored him or maybe he never called.

After the furniture store, I worked in the office at St. John's for a couple of weeks. I was sitting in for someone else. The priests were friends of our family, so we helped them when we could.

College and Dates

"Parents can only give good advice or put them on the
right paths, but the final forming of a person's
character lies in their own hands."
—Anne Frank

The day finally came. I was starting college with a future
degree in something I didn't choose but was decided for me.

My transportation was the city bus and soon I began taking
Sears driving lessons.

Finding a new hairdresser and dating the owner.

Dating others, I had no interest in.

I started attending classes and soon found part-time work in
the Administration offices, running errands between departments.
Not much later, I was assigned to the Health Department where
I was one of two Administrators. We copied exams on a ditto
machine. It was a small machine with a round cylinder that was
cranked to roll the papers that needed to be copied. We also had
foils. These were very thin plastic sheets used for presentations
that were placed on a projector to project onto a big white screen.

My degree should have been in Interior Design, but Mom
had other ideas. One day, I said to her, "I want to be an interior

designer." "Oh no!" Mom says, just like that! "Why can't you just study to be a secretary?"

That is not what I wanted to hear. I went back to thinking what else there could be and finally decided to take Bilingual Business classes and see where that took me. My parents agreed. It is strange that I needed their approval for my future endeavors, but I was always afraid to start issues. That is why today, I listen to me and do what I desire. Even today, there are activities I enjoy, and Mom thinks they are silly and a waste of time.

When I signed up for my first semester, I added a few art classes, just in case my parents changed their minds. Dad paid for my first semester.

There were challenges during the first few years because I didn't drive so I had to take the city bus. I refused to let Dad teach me how to drive. He was very impatient when training my siblings. I preferred to save to pay someone else.

One time while transferring to another bus, I was crossing the street, a drunk man began harassing me and thank God I was saved by another stranger who recognized me from other days. He was clean and sober. He walked next to me and stayed until I got on the next bus.

Another time I got on the wrong bus, and it was the last run of the evening. I ended up at the bus depot. The bus driver knew I was frightened so he called me up to the front and handed me a roll of nickels and then took me into their office so I could call Dad. I hated to call because I knew there was a big chance, I would put him in a bad mood but fortunately, this time he was more worried than angry.

I finally saved enough money to take Sears driving classes. I had no car, so Dad let me drive his old car and he drove an even older truck that Uncle Bud gave him. The first mistake I made was to leave the car in neutral. When I left work and walked to the parking lot, I found that the car had rolled down and was right in the middle of a path that makes it easier to get to the main street. It was blocking the cars from going through. There were very few cars left and I'm sure many drivers who had to take an alternative route were sitting at home talking about that dumb driver!

Starting a new life, I had to find a new hairdresser, plus Renae, my last hairdresser had moved out of her home. Ana found a salon by the University of Arizona. It wasn't on campus but very close. It was called Michael the Crimper's. Michael was the owner; he cut my hair if the other hairdresser was not available.

Michael asked me out to dinner. He was about 42 and I was 18. My immediate thought was, "What would my parents think?" I told him I'd let him know.

"Oh, he's an older man! He's nice. Let her go. It's just dinner!" This is Ana convincing our parents.

Michael shows up in sandals and carrying a small, beaded satchel. He had blond, shoulder-length, curly hair. Dad thought he was gay so was super fine with me going!

We went to Bobby McGee's. It was in the opposite side of town, as East as you can get. When walking to the door of the restaurant, Michael stops to pick a flower from a nearby bush and places it in my hair over my right ear. I was so shy that I wish I could remember how I felt and what our conversation was about. He took me home and that was that. I continued seeing him and the other hairdresser for my hair care until I got married and left Tucson.

Years later, when we returned to Tucson, I was told he no longer had his salon but that the other guy was working out of his home. My sister gave me his number and so I made an appointment. The first time he was normal, was on time, and did a great job. The second time, he was late, came in smelling like pot and while washing my hair, he kept talking about a book he was reading. It involved murders and slicing of necks, and my neck is hanging in the basin and I'm freaking out. I never went back and neither did my sister. He was getting too strange. Not sure what my sister's reason was for leaving him.

This must have been the year of dates. I went to a drive-in movie with a friend from school. We watched *Jaws*. That night

I had nightmares but not because of the movie. I saw the guy's teeth chomping in circles. I didn't date him for long.

My neighbor, Veronica, and I went to ball games to watch her boyfriend play. This is where I met another man wanting to be my boyfriend, but he wasn't my type. My parents loved him. He and Dad sat at the kitchen table in conversation, with me wishing he'd leave. He wrote me poems and mailed them to me even after I brushed him off. His mom also loved me and was knitting me a sweater. Poor lady, hopefully she found someone to give it to.

Making New Routines

"Everything you are used to, once done long enough, starts to seem natural, even though it might not be."
—Julien Smith

During the first semester, a teacher took our bilingual class to Hermosillo. It was a student exchange. This was also a lesson of the maquiladoras. The maquiladoras are U.S. (or other country) manufacturing companies in Mexico. They export the products back to the U.S. or owner's country. I don't remember much about this trip except that I made friends and the only reason I know is because I found a letter in that "Personal" folder from one of the girls. She references another girl and my Tía Chata who had moved to Hermosillo from Rayón. I am guessing that I took them to my tía's home to introduce them. I do recall being excited to go home to get my license, finally!

I had just turned 19 when we returned from Hermosillo when Gloria took me to get my driver's license. She is explaining the tests I will face, not paying attention to where she was going. As we turn into the parking lot, she hits one of the instructor's cars, with him in it. We slowly get out of the car to see the damage. We were relieved that it was minimal and hardly noticeable. She got away with it and something we laughed about all the way home.

While working in the Health Department, I worked with Polina, a dental professor who came from Russia. She loved the clothes Mom made me, so she used mom for alterations of clothes she bought. Mom became her seamstress and interestingly, they never met. It was always business through me.

Polina and I went to Nogales, Sonora, because she was going to make a presentation at a school and leaving donated dental material. She knew of a restaurant (La Roca) that served great margaritas. We stopped on our way home. By the time it was time to leave, she couldn't safely drive us home, so she had me drive — in the dark. I was not yet comfortable driving. I didn't own a car, so I didn't have enough driving experience. When driving, I kept steering towards the shoulder near the freeway exits and fortunately I'd catch myself before driving right into the rails. This happened all the way into Tucson. It was a nightmare. She mentioned we'd go on another trip, but I prayed she'd forget, and she did!

During the second semester is when I began working in the evenings at the car dealership. This place was an experience. Used-car salesmen are the worse! They were all in their 50's and older. They also sold new cars, but I liked referring to them as the used-car salesmen.

The same salesman that coerced me to talk to Dad, that one evening when I was angry with Dad and I wouldn't thank him for driving me to work, was also the one who taught me that chewing gum did not look attractive on women and in my position, I should not chew gum. To this day, the only time I chew gum is when I go for long walks. When I see others chewing gum, I want to reach out and tell them how ugly it looks.

Another time Tony, a new friend who had just moved from New York, came by to pick me up. We were going to a party at a friends' home. When he walked in, the salesmen checked him out head to toe and some teased him about taking me with him. The next evening, they tell me to be careful with boys like him. I never dated Tony. He was just a friend and I trusted him. The salesmen should speak for themselves. I watched as they stared at women as they shopped for cars. Afterwards, they'd gather around and make rude comments and laugh! Sometimes their behavior was embarrassing and uncomfortable.

Working at Pima during the six years, was a busy time. I liked being away from home. It was my time of freedom, but I was also working myself thin. I took classes in the early mornings, worked full-time during the days, and then the evening job. At lunch I played racquetball. The racquetball courts were outside in the heat. Sometimes we jogged on the desert trails no matter how hot it was. The heat never bothered me until I got much older.

I also enrolled in Bailes Folkorico, a Mexican dance class with Professor Angel. We had practices right after work and sometimes on weekends. He used to tease me about my crooked knees and worked to get me to straighten out. I finally learned the steps and was allowed to participate in recitals that took us from the Tucson Community Center to many surrounding towns in Arizona.

We had to make our own dresses. Some of the dresses took many yards of fabric and when the dress was finished, it weighed a ton! We also had to make our own props. One of them was a decorated cross. We were given the measurements and the color of ribbon to buy. Working every day, I had Saturday to buy what I needed. I was still working on the cross on Sunday. The recital was at 5 that evening, but we had to be there earlier. I told Dad I was going to skip mass and he tells me that I can't skip it and he sends me off. I don't know what good that did because I was so worried that I wouldn't have time to decorate the cross. I get home in a hurry only to find that Dad had finished it for me. Dad was already on his way to recovery both physically and spiritually. He had a good heart. He was so happy to see the surprise and thankful look on my face. Dad drove us to the recital and he and Mom stayed to watch me dance.

I continued dancing and performing for about four years. I became good friends with Angel even when he got very sick with throat cancer. I took him Shaklee supplements, popular then, in both powder and capsules. He wanted to be cured but nothing worked. He finally left for Mexico to be with his family for the last few months of his life.

During one of my last visits with him, he gifted me with a silver coin. I treasured that coin for years until someone ransacked our home in San Diego and took it with many other valuables. I don't need materialistic things to remember him by. I will always remember him for accepting me into the group and for becoming a friend I could trust.

After Angel passed away, it wasn't the same anymore, but I hung in. My knees were beginning to give me problems. I figured it was from all the practices and recitals, but I continued dancing.

Figure 1 Sylvia with the Pima Community College Bailes Folklorico.

Rheumatoid Arthritis

"Pain is such an uncomfortable feeling that even a tiny amount of it is enough to ruin every enjoyment."
—*Will Rogers*

Who would have thought that a simple pain would change the rest of my life?

The joy of school and activities ended that year, at least temporarily.

The future involved trials and disappointments, and not temporarily.

The future also meant I had to prove myself against what people suggested or came right out to tell me, including the doctors.

During Christmas break of my second year, in 1975, it was the evening before Christmas Eve. Gloria and I planned to go to a Christmas party. Mom was complaining that I was going out so late and should be focusing on the real purpose of Christmas. Stubborn as I was, I still made plans. I was taking a nap and was just going to get up to take a shower — and couldn't get out of bed. My back hurt badly. I had to go to the restroom, so I forced myself out of bed and crawled to the restroom. I could see the fear in my parents' eyes, even Dad's. I tried not to make it look so painful, but I couldn't hide it. Dad took me to the hospital. After a few tests, they found I had a kidney infection; I was told to visit our family doctor as soon as they opened after the holidays.

I didn't go to the party and felt badly for Gloria who had everything planned out. My fingers and knees began to hurt. By the time I saw the doctor, I was in pain all over my body. I also developed hives. The doctor also diagnosed the kidney infection, but his bigger concern were the body pains. He found out I was borderline Lupus and likely had Rheumatoid Arthritis. I couldn't hold a pen and became very fatigued. The doctor asked me to stop all my physical activities.

As I was walking out of the doctor's office, I noticed all the elderly people waiting, and witnessed the deformity on their hands and feet. It scared me enough, so I reluctantly stopped my activities, and started taking the medication. It took three months before the medication kicked in. I went back to my activities as soon as the pain subsided. When the doctor saw that I was doing well he praised me for disobeying his orders to stop the activities.

I didn't understand the consequences RA would have on my life going forward until the pain strikes again and again. It's like you feel great and then the weather changes or your body reacts to some unexpected drama and the pain returns. I also found out that people look at me as if I am perfectly fine because I have no outer signs of RA. RA is also a cause for fatigue. Imagine hurting and keeping it within and the pain continues day after day, and you continue to function like a person without it. It is double the effort and no one seems to care or understand. My husband sees when my pain comes and when it goes so, I think he understands. Laurie and Ana suffer their own, so we support each other.

I continued taking some courses. The one that I most enjoyed was Spanish Literature. I took it for two semesters. I learned how to write stories in Spanish. Professor Mendez was my professor and my inspiration. I had a couple of my stories published in one of the Llueve Tlotlec magazines that reside in the Pima College library archives. I have a copy that I saved and occasionally I read my stories and remember how I dreamed in Spanish when writing in Spanish.

During the time I temporarily stopped all physical activity, Suzanne, my peer, and friend, liked to hang outside of the office to check out the scene, mainly boys. There was a cement wall around the whole campus on the second floor but low enough to jump onto it to sit (and not get caught), or just to lean on.

There was one very good-looking black guy I had my eye on. He was taking a Photography class. I shied away from him and any guy that looked at me because of my hair and lips. My hair was at its longest. I was very thin. Mom used to say that I could probably wear my bra backwards because my shoulder bones stuck out. This one day, while we are leaning on the wall, he comes up to me and whispers in my ear, "I need a winning picture. I'd like to put you on a horse in the nude!" He left me speechless. Then I shouted, "Never, and don't ever ask again!" and he walks away chuckling. He continued coming by to taunt me.

Another time as I'm gracefully walking down the stairs to get to the library, there is a group of guys at the bottom of the stairs. One of them is my photography friend. There is another guy in crutches who lives a couple of streets from our street. There was a group of about four guys. They watch as I walk down, one calling out, "luscious lips," and my dear photography friend saying, "She won't let me take her picture!" He knew better to not repeat what he had asked earlier.

The guy in the crutches asked me out but I declined. I was too embarrassed to take anyone home. I was embarrassed of myself.

Later, this same photography guy met me at a wedding. Mom and Dad must have known the parents of the bride or groom. They sat behind us. When at home Dad began to tease me about being with a black guy. I was in total shock and so I asked him where that talk came from. He backed off realizing he was in the wrong. This is the first time that racism came so close to home. He never mentioned it again.

I met a guy at a quinceañera. At the end of the celebration, he asked me on a date. I accepted and my parents were livid.

They knew something about him but weren't telling me. The day he came to pick me up Dad told me that if I insisted on dating him, he would never be allowed into our home. He came once and was not allowed in. Mom and I thought Dad had gone too far. But I was rebelling and continued seeing him.

My poor brothers had to endure being our chaperones when we started dating, much older than 15. Now that I think about it, it was only with select guys. I remember going on some dates without the chaperone, but we were given strict instructions to be home by a certain time. However, I always needed a chaperone with this guy.

He was into car racing and the only restaurant he ever took me to was McDonalds. My friends saw what I couldn't see or refused to see. He didn't work so I figured he didn't have money to go to college so I made him promise he would go to his classes if I paid for his first semester. No one knew I paid for a small schedule of classes. I found out later that he wasn't attending them.

Gloria has a cousin who was good friends with a guy they thought would be perfect for me. They planned a weekend of going out to bars and dancing and that's where I met my future husband. He was my blind date. I broke up with the other guy and he became angry and followed me for a year. I'd find him waiting for me at my car kicking at my tires begging me to get back with him. However, it was over, and my parents were happy that I finally left him.

After all the physical suffering from the RA, I no longer had a desire to continue my education at a University. I also dropped some classes at Pima College, especially shorthand. The handwriting resulted in my fingers swelling and was very painful.

After six years of taking advantage of classes while I worked at Pima College, I graduated with 105 credits. Teachers tried to accommodate me so that I could finish the last two classes I needed to get the Bilingual Business degree. I didn't have it in me so instead I graduated with a General Studies Associate of Arts degree.

Shortly before I ended my studies at the college, I experienced the unexpected. I was asked to temporarily take on the responsibilities of the President's assistant while the assistant was on medical leave. In that position, I was asked to type the President's speech for the graduation to be held that evening. Unbeknownst to him, I was also graduating. When the professors and the President stood on the stage to congratulate each graduate, the President was very surprised when he saw me walk up to the stage. He gave me a hug and whispered in my ear, "Why didn't you tell me you were graduating?"

He then made a special announcement to thank me for typing his speech and congratulated me once more in front of the audience. This was one event I will never forget. I felt very special. My parents were there to witness this gesture and were very proud. It was so good to see my Dad grinning ear to ear!

For many years, I harbored the disappointment of not receiving a Business Degree and continuing to a university. I regret this more than anything in my life!

I continued working at Pima College. I had since been moved to the Bilingual and International Studies Department, working as the Admin for the Dean. He kept extremely busy and so I was busy.

He was a presenter at workshops and conferences. Sometimes he traveled out of the country. During one of those travels, he called. That evening, I had fallen asleep reading a book. The ring of the phone woke me up, it was around 10 p.m. I picked up the receiver and began talking about the book. It was like sleep talking. The dean's voice then became clear, and I fully awoke. I was speaking nonsense, and he asked what time it was, apologized and hung up. He probably needed something done for an early meeting.

He was a very strict man. He corrected anyone who called him "Mr." and expected me to enforce his correct name. I made sure anyone who came into his office referred to him as "Dean". He must have approved of my services because he trusted me enough to be sent to Mexico City to lead a group of 11 non-Spanish speaking students and one other who knew some Spanish was the daughter of a family friend. We were to study Art and the History of Mexico. The trip was for a month.

Gloria, my high school friend and I, had traveled to Guadalajara a year earlier for a week. We traveled by train. The train ran out of water in the middle of the summer. We drank whatever was available, even beer. The stay was fun but hard to understand the Spanish dialect that we weren't familiar with. It was like the words were sung. We watched and listened to many mariachi groups, and we shopped. It was a good short vacation and nothing unusual happened other than the train ride.

So, when the dean had mentioned the trip to Mexico, I immediately thought back to the train ride and the language I thought to myself, *"What more can happen in Mexico!"*

On this trip, we were placed with different families. A family member took each of us to school and picked us up. My family consisted of a daughter older than I and a young man about my age, the single mom, and a maid.

The son was a dedicated soccer player. After playing soccer, his mom rubbed his legs with marijuana oil. That was new to me! He was also a dedicated partier! We did a lot of partying on weekends.

During the week we studied, helped with meals, and washed our clothes. Washing our clothes was an ordeal. We washed what we could since the washer was small and we had lots of clothes! We hung the washed clothes on the clothesline outside on the balcony. It constantly sprinkled or rained, so many times our clothes were damp. We had to bring them inside and hang them on furniture to finish the drying.

The first time we were served rice and bananas for dinner, we could not stop laughing. That was rude of us, but the banana was just so random and looked so funny on the plate. The "bananas" were plantains and were delicious. We didn't laugh the second time around!

We learned to salsa dance, and we visited surrounding pueblos. We bought lots of souvenirs even though we didn't know how we'd fit them in our already stuffed suitcases. I didn't have to worry much because at the end of the trip, some of my clothes went missing.

On the night before the last day, a few of us from my class went out. Beto, the guy from our family, picked everyone up and stuffed us into his Volkswagen. He and his friends had been smoking pot. I don't recall what Beto did that caused the police to pull him over. We ended up in jail while they settled on a fine. They didn't put us behind bars, instead we sat on chairs facing a wall. Pretty soon, we saw cockroaches crawling on the walls. The whole situation was creepy and scary. We went home that night in silence.

The next morning when we arrived at school, the first sight was a couple of painters painting the exterior walls. "School is over," they shouted at us as we got closer to the front door. "It was over yesterday at noon." Oops! How did we miss that! We thanked the painters and left while they cursed, called us a few names and laughed at us.

When we are back in Tucson, our grades were passed out. Afraid to look, I was pleased to see that I was given a "B" for the two classes. What a relief and I know that the dean had something to do with it!

I also stopped working my evening job but not until I bought my first car. A couple of the salesmen helped me pick one out that I could comfortably afford. I chose a Volare! My husband teases me about that car. "What is a Volare?" I never saw another one in my life. We gave it to my brother Jerry and have no idea what he did with it.

The Interview

*"Sometimes beautiful things come into our lives out
of nowhere. We can't always understand them, but we
must trust in them. I know you want to question everything, but sometimes it pays to just have a little faith.*
—Lauren Kate

After six years at the Junior College, I was given the opportunity to begin my corporate experience. One day, I heard
the dean in a conversation with his assistant. He asked her to
recommend me for an opening at a large corporation. I didn't
know it existed nor did I know there was a big plant in Tucson.
Within a week, I had been recommended and was asked to go
in for an interview. I had to quickly learn about the company,
and I still didn't comprehend that I was interviewing with one
of the largest and most successful global companies.

As I recall, the interview wasn't frightening and now when I
think back, it's probably because I knew so little of it and didn't
feel intimidated. Had I known more about the company and
what I know today, I would have worried.

To this day, there is only one question that sticks in my head.
They asked numerous times if I was flexible. I quickly said I was,

not knowing what it meant for my future. They were interested in me, and I was hired. Believe me, you must be flexible to work at this company because everything constantly changes; it could be your responsibilities, the systems you use, or the policies you must abide by. Plus, you must constantly adjust to new management!

The staff at the college held a going-away luncheon for me. As a gift to the dean, I gave him a small leather whip in a fancy box. The dean was demanding but what a good person he was. I used to tease him that all he needed was a whip to keep us all straight. When he opened the gift, he was like a little kid. He thought it was the best gift ever. He kept it on display on his desk, I was told.

One of the coaches that saw me at racquetball or out jogging, always yelled out, "Cecilia, how's it going?" and started singing "Oh Cecilia, you're breaking my heart." I ignored the name and just smiled at him, and we'd go our separate ways. At the party is when he finds out what my real name is. After six years, I told him my real name!! I explained that I wished I was given that name instead of Sylvia. He gave me a big hug and we said our good-byes.

The dean and his assistant believed in me and saw what I didn't see. I never thought that another place existed for me. I will forever be grateful for the two of them.

PART TWO

Twenty Plus Years of Work-Life Unbalanced

"You gain strength, courage, and confidence by every experience in which you really stop to look fear in the face. You must do the thing you think you cannot do."
—Eleanor Roosevelt

It was in the next 20+ years that I had to learn to come out of my shell. I had to become the employee I wanted to be. The one whom my managers and peers could count on. I worked hard and I played hard.

I learned more about being flexible, moving from one location to another, and one department to another.

New positions meant meeting new people and challenges. Meeting the people who were labeled the outcasts or scary ones — and making them my friends. Breaking the arrogance out of some was my personal challenge and at the end, I learned that no matter how high up a ladder a person is, they are also human, just like me.

Getting close to people and then they die and are no longer there for me.

Getting engaged only after threatening to break up and then moving to San Diego where moving challenges occurred and again new personalities to learn.

I grew more, I tolerated more but I also learned more about discrimination. I learned from my mistakes.

I learned that mistakes are lessons that sometimes bring awards because someone recognized your potential and intentions.

I learned from training the company provided. Traveling for education and finding people look at you as if you are from another planet.

Having to go unemployed, not by choice. Moving again, this time with a child.

Mourning for the work life, fighting depression, and learning to live with disappointment. Rejoining the workforce, this time with the fear of leaving our child with strangers, people who are not her color, a worry even in our generation.

New work in Colorado, same company; only a quite different environment, jealousy, more racism this time accidentally, that I was not supposed to hear.

Finding daycare at a home because the first daycare didn't like brown girls or the bald girl battling leukemia.

Pushed to my limits, suicide became a thought but instead, I resigned. I rested until I was strong and courageous to attempt work at a place that was not a big corporation. The first attempt at an interview sickened me.

The new day-to-day routine, how relaxing and easy it was but soon I was bored. The good news, I had the opportunity to help at Melissa's kindergarten and part of her first grade.

The big corporation calls me back. I accept only to find myself in another new environment, facing a hysterectomy and coming back to a new manager.

Once again, we move. This time it's to go home. Parents aging, so we must go.

Corporate Experience Begins

"God is so good to give us new days and New Years since He knows we need so many times to start over."
—Lacey Sturm

On my first day, March 3, 1980, I wore a pretty lime-green dress with a matching jacket. It was snug, a little above the knee and a V-neck and high heels. My hair was a little below my shoulders, now a darker brown. I remember having to park at least half a mile from the entrance. There were a few construction workers at a building to my right. I was walking, as straight as could be with my head up high, so proud of going into work on this first day. I was dressed nice and looked professional. The whistling and comments that were directed at me by the construction workers quickly interrupted the happiness and security I felt. I still had at least a quarter mile to go and wanted so much for the ground to swallow me. I was never so devastated. I could just hear Mom saying,

"That's what you get for being so proud."

But on this day, no one was going to bring me down.

When I finally arrived at my desk I was introduced to my principals, those I would support. One of them came up to me and blurted out an apology for the construction workers. I was embarrassed that he had heard and seen it all. I am sure that he too was enjoying my walk all the way to the office.

And this is where it all began. My first position at this company was as an Administrative Assistant. In my naïve mind, I thought that my future was about doing a great job to advance. As a minority, I always felt like I had to work twice as hard as my counterparts. I also carried the thoughts of having to take special classes in high school and that I didn't have a four-year college degree. I never gave myself credit for the skills I learned working at Pima College, degree, or no degree. I appreciated the 12 years of Catholic schools that our parents sent us to with many sacrifices. In those years, Catholic schools on a resume were a bonus I doubt it is today.

I supported a few managers. They all treated me well and very quickly I was receiving praises and raises. The first raise was a jump to $12/hour, something unheard of in Tucson at that time (1980's). I was stunned and proud at the same time when my manager presented me with the raise.

During my earlier time at this company, I played softball with a group of people in the department. I was put on 1st base and was eventually called "stretch." I didn't move much around the base but with stretched arm I caught the ball almost every time. Most were women I supported.

One lady was dating one of the males I supported. I didn't know she was dating him. I enjoyed watching him when he'd come into the office to pick up his mail. I'd also see him without his girlfriend at a country bar that Gloria and I went to. We were in our 20's, so we were beyond the 18 years of legal drinking. I never danced with him, but being young and silly, we just looked and giggled! A few months later he was in a car accident and passed away.

There was another guy in our department that watched us play. He had bone cancer but was still getting around. When we had practice on Saturdays, he invited us over for breakfast and to use his pool as we wished. Nice guy, but he didn't last long either.

It was getting creepy that everyone I liked was passing before me. What kind of a sign was that?

The softball ended for me when it became coed. I was afraid I'd not be good enough. They were stronger and I was afraid that catching a male's strong throw would hurt my arthritic hands. I couldn't risk getting injured.

There was a position for a promotion and knowing that all my reviews were high on the scale, and the managers I supported gave my managers good feedback, I confidently expressed my interest. When someone with less experience was offered the position, I didn't know what to think. Yes, it bothered me, but I was too new to this world and so I brushed it off and kept the faith that a promotion would come my way very soon. She was in my department, and it was simply reorganizing the department.

It was at this first location that I met one of my best friends, Kathi, who has remained dear to me. The good overpowered the disappointment! She was the one I went to when I faced disappointment, and she did the same in turning to me. During one Halloween we dressed as bunnies, and we did a really great job, bunny ears and teeth to boot! Two silly girls and now two silly old ladies! We have not changed a bit!

I didn't get the position but instead I was moved to the Airport Site. It was great because it was much closer to home. I used to get drowsy driving to and from work. The evening sun was the worst.

My responsibilities didn't change except that I became the backup to the plant manager's secretary. He was a fun man. He kept finding his jellybean jar low or empty. He decided to put tape around his door to see if he could figure out when in the day, they were taken. He was at his desk all day and if he slipped out for a meeting, we were there to keep watch, and so we determined the jellybeans were taken at night. We found out it was the custodian. The manager continued bringing larger bags to have enough for himself and the custodian!

Another pet peeve of this plant manager was a pair of pants I wore. They were an olive green, baggy with elastic at the ankles.

I wore them with a waist length sheer black blouse with large red roses and lime green leaves. I thought I looked nice! In fact, it was one of my best outfits. Each time I'd wear them he would say, "When you take those pants off, bring them to me so I can put them on my bulletin board and throw darts at them!" He had something against these pants!

While working in this department, I supported programmers and engineers. I was told to expect it to be boring because the group didn't talk much! There was one programmer who was pointed out as being rude and that his looks would scare me. When I met him, I only saw that he had long hair and a beard and didn't think he was scary. He didn't say a word to me when we were introduced.

I always have a way of getting involved with people others can't handle, fear, or dislike or are simply rude. This programmer became a valuable pal. He helped me learn how to use a system to get to my email, later he taught me how use a database for keeping track of programmers' data. It wasn't day after day but the time he spent with me was priceless. We even went on walks during lunch.

I had already dated my husband for six years before he had moved to San Diego to begin his Engineering career. I thought it was odd that he had not proposed. He had sent me a dozen roses that I wasn't acknowledging. I even accepted a dinner with a man from the original plant I had started at. I wasn't interested in this man, but he asked me to dinner, and I thought it wouldn't hurt and went with him. When I got home Mom made me call him to thank him for the roses. Then one weekend he unexpectedly, arrived to propose sooner than he had anticipated.

"You just couldn't wait!" he told me after he proposed!

I didn't stay long at this facility after I got engaged. I transferred to the San Diego branch office. Everyone was jealous and I was excited to start a new adventure. Kathi was sad but she too was soon engaged and eventually moved to Atlanta. When we both need a laugh, we get on the phone and laugh at the past and the new memories we are making.

We married on April 16, 1982, a month after I moved to San Diego.
Ralph was already living and working there.

So happy to have grandparents at our wedding.
It was not easy for them to travel from Mexico.

Dad as Deacon with priest.

First San Diego Position

"The secret of life is not to do what you like,
but to like what you do."
—Anonymous

I moved to San Diego in March of 1982 because the branch needed me to start on March 1st. Well, not being married, my parents wouldn't hear of me staying with my future husband. They decided to contact a friend of theirs, a couple who were strangers to me. They arranged that I would stay with them until we got married. That was fine but didn't they worry that just because I slept at this stranger's house didn't mean that I wouldn't be visiting my fiancé during the day and who knows what we would be doing! All was good. The people I stayed with were very personable and made me feel welcome. We got married on April 16, 1982, in Tucson, and moved to our first apartment in San Diego a week later.

My first position was in Word Processing. The room was separate from the large open area, the desks were side by side.

Entering the building was not like the Tucson office needing badges to enter every room; instead, they had an old, retired security guard.

The day before, I had missed a marital fight that I understood went like this: There were two engineers who were seeing each other but married (or separated) from other people. The wife of the male engineer got past security with a pie in her hand. She walked directly over to the husband and/or the female engineer and threw the pie in their face. After that incident, a new badge system was implemented.

During my Word Processing days, shortly after arriving I was sent to Los Angeles to learn a new word processor. It was nerve wracking having to learn how to get to LA. My husband was nice to take me on a drive the weekend before the class to figure out the route. Since he was working, I had to drive myself on the day of class. All was good!

I learned all about the Mag Card, and Boiler Plates that were used as templates for the sales proposals. Lily, the Word Processor Administrator who was there before me, taught me the basics. She warned me of the late nights that occurred right before the quarter closes when the sales reps are bringing in last-minute sales. She was right. There were days that would turn into nights while we typed away with the sales reps leaning on our chairs anxiously waiting for the finished copy. They proofed as we typed. It wasn't stressful, especially when the reps bribed us and bought us drinks at happy hour or brought us gifts.

One day I caught my peer suspiciously drinking from a thermos. Then she shares it is orange juice and vodka. No one ever caught her. I never tried it, but occasionally we had wine with our lunch. We knew it was prohibited but it wasn't as strict as it became later. I know we were bad, so don't do this. It's not a good example!

My Word Processing manager was thrilled to have me. It was the beginning of March when I transferred and on April 1st, I sent her a long note stating how much I enjoyed her and the work and that I was sorry that I needed to resign, and I kept going on and on until at the very end I wrote, "April Fools." My peer couldn't believe I did this being so new in the office. Fortunately, our manager had a sense of humor. She shared it with everyone for a very long time and eventually it got old!

During this time, I met friends I would have to this day. One of them, Josephine, was pretty and very smart. She was sitting in a corner cubicle outside of Word Processing. She had on a suit and what caught my attention was a big white bow tie. She had beautiful long hair and was about my height. She is the one who introduced me to Ann, an older woman who was about to retire. We all became close friends. Ann worked in Word Processing for a few months.

A couple of weeks later, our manager came into Word Processing asking for Ann. Her husband was waiting right outside the door. The door was closed but we could still hear the commotion! Turns out that Bob had planned a trip to Hawaii for Ann's birthday. He had packed her suitcase and was picking her up on the way to the airport. Ann was beyond surprised and even more surprised when she was told she'd be gone for a week. This meant that Bob had already cleared the vacation with her manager.

Soon after, Josephine who introduced me to Ann, married Conrado, who also worked with us in another department. They married and left San Diego. I was sorry to see her leave and didn't think I would ever see her again.

Lily, my Word Processing peer, introduced me to her cousin, Cierra, whom I still see when we visit San Diego. Her daughter is our Goddaughter. Cierra and her cousin are Guamanian. They shared Guamanian food with us, and we shared Mexican food with them. They became our second family.

Cierra was in Accounts Receivable (A/R). She introduced me to her friends, Liz who has a New Jersey accent, and Austin. They all worked together. Three or four of us regularly had lunch together. Since our office was right on Hotel Circle, we had many restaurant options.

Going to lunch with the A/R group gave me the desire to move out of Word Processing. From listening to Cierra and Austin's discussions of their day-to-day responsibilities and working with the Sales Reps and customers, made my days look boring. They were responsible for ensuring the customers paid their invoices. They also worked with the Customer Support Representatives (CSRs). The CSRs had a variety of tasks they were responsible for. Challenges and multi-tasking are what I enjoyed. This position was more down my alley and that's the move I was working for. The move to the CSR position didn't happen immediately. I stayed in Word Processing for about a year.

Administrative Assistant

"Do not fear the thorns in your path,
for they draw only corrupt blood.
—Khalil Gibran

I was then moved to the Sales side of the business with a new title and a raise, but it was not a promotion. I became an Administrative Assistant, supporting Sales Managers, Software and Services Managers and their Sales Representatives. My desk was in an open area with offices on one side and the Sales Reps and Software and Services Reps in the open area. I sat next to the Branch Manager's secretary and right next to the copier and fax machine.

It was initially challenging, having to learn everyone's personalities. Sometimes I felt like I was babysitting; other times I felt like the wife; and other times like the Branch Manager's secretary assistant.

I was reprimanded for asking the custodian to restock the toilet paper bin after a rep came storming out of the restroom complaining that it was empty. Then I was yelled at for mentioning the rep's name as being the one complaining. I didn't mention it. It was just assumed.

I was also the eyes for the Branch Manager assistant. She had problems seeing and refused to wear bifocals. When the Branch Manager needed a phone number, she'd shout for me to give it to her, then she'd dial the number for him. She also told me I had a cute nose. That was so random. I picked up lunch for the managers if they knew a conference call or a meeting was going to run through lunch.

Another time, a sales rep who was diagnosed with colon cancer, asked me to be her witness on a will she was preparing for her daughter and the person who would be assigned her guardian. It was the saddest request. She became thinner, and the thinner she became, the prettier clothes she wore. She wore expensive knit dresses that revealed her curves. During her last summer she wore colorful flowy skirts with matching shirts. The belts are what I loved. The colors were of the brightest colors and that is what caught my attention. She wore beautiful expensive jewelry that was included in her will She was a top seller but didn't get the chance to make it far. And when she passed, everyone felt her loss.

A few months before she passed away and before anyone knew she was sick she came to my desk to ask for a request. As we are speaking, she looked at me and told me I looked very pretty with the lipstick I was wearing. It was a mauve color and she pointed out that the red I had worn earlier was not a good shade for me. She said it in a very kind and gentle way. I was not used to compliments so I took her advice to heart. Many years later I had my lips tattooed in mauve.

There was one Sales Rep who was one of the most successful in sales. He was handsome and the rudest. It took a dream to get him to soften up and be more open with me. I dreamed that I was looking for him in Pluto and when I found him, he was ignoring me, but I needed to give him customer information and he kept ignoring me. When I told him about it, I saw his smile for the first time. He began to small talk to me, and I appreciated it more than his prior rudeness. He gave me assignments that he wouldn't have before.

I also dreamed I was picking up laundry for the managers. I had so many dreams that I began writing them and still do.

The loud copier was driving me nuts and deaf. The fax machine was the other one I fought with. It never seemed to work properly, and it was frustrating when managers needed important documents "wired" right away. "Wired" is how the sending of a fax was referred to at that time (early '80s). Managers would ask I "wire" a document to headquarters or to the manufacturing plants. Paul, who was quite older and possibly could have been my grandfather, was one of the easiest-going persons. He knew how much I fought with the fax machine, so he came over with his hands behind his back. He kneeled and presented me with a bent paper clip. "Would you please wire this?" he asked! He made me laugh each time. It didn't get old because it was him!

Cierra lived close to his apartment and saw him looking very lonely. His wife had recently passed away. Bless their hearts. With this man I learned to have some fun at work and not be so serious.

While in this position, I had a couple of opportunities of wining and dining after receiving awards for working overtime to complete a large project or just for outstanding support. Spouses were invited to these dinners, something that rarely happens today.

Our Branch Manager was a Mormon and although he didn't drink, he ordered wine or champagne for the table. The restaurants were 5-star restaurants. We always enjoyed these events with him.

On another occasion Jake, another Administrator and I, were awarded a trip to the Olympics basketball games held in Los Angeles. We joined the Sales Reps and the Technical group. We sat together on the bus and at the event. On the way back from the Olympics we found lunch boxes on our seats. We were told that someone will walk by to collect any leftover and empty boxes. A techie sat in front of us. He was big and needed both seats. He kept both lunch boxes and ate one of them quickly. When the lady walked by, he handed her the empty box. We looked at each other and wanted to laugh out loud but we kept it quiet until the bus drove off. We could not stop laughing. I've had these uncontrollable laughs at work a few times.

Becoming A Customer Support Rep

> *"By three methods we may learn wisdom:*
> *First by reflection, which is noblest; second,*
> *by imitation, which is easiest; and third by experience,*
> *which is the bitterest."*
> —*Confuscius*

In 1984, shortly after our Olympics trip, I applied for a Customer Support Rep (CSR) position, and it was offered to me. This was my first promotion. This was a delight! It felt like a personal acknowledgement that I was on that right path in my journey to succeed. With great confidence I accepted the promotion knowing that it may present new challenges, but I was ready for them. I had to demonstrate to my bosses and support group that I had something to offer but truly was not sure what it was.

I was moved to what they called a "bull pen" where I joined Cierra and my other lunch buddies. There were about four Customer Service Reps plus the Accounts Receivable group. There were no walls separating us. It was hard speaking to customers when we were hearing each other's voices. Then we had to deal with personalities and some pet peeves, like the tapping on the shoulder or the pushing of the elbow to get our attention. Then we had the one employee who constantly looked over our shoulder. I could tune him out, but it irritated Cierra, causing her to make the nastiest faces and that entertained the rest of us!

I was trained by a senior CSR, who was very thorough and repeated everything a hundred times. For nights I had dreams of her index finger pointing at the computer or of her telling me I should keep my voice down and not to visit with my peers. She also mentioned not to get too friendly with our customers. I was already nervous about this position. I was going to embark into a new environment! Even though I was trained by one of the senior peers, most of my education happened through experience and sometimes it wasn't in the most pleasant way.

I became friends with some of our customers. We met for lunch after discussing five minutes of business or we met for drinks and usually they were just part of our office happy hours. For years I didn't understand why the sales managers didn't question our friendship with the customers but now I know that it was benefitting them! They were some of our best customers buying our products, so why change it?

I was initially assigned small customers. This I was thankful for, because the orders were small, and I needed to understand everything about sales, from receiving the order to entering the order, and then following up with the shipment and delivery, and putting the hardware on maintenance. If the customer was behind in payment, I worked between the A/R person and the customer until payments were caught up.

During this time, it was easy for our manager to find backup when I was sent to Atlanta two times, sometimes for two weeks at a time. The first time I went alone to learn all about the CSR responsibilities and how the position interacted with many parts of the business. We had people from the plants and Atlanta headquarters providing training. It was nice to meet them face to face rather than just by phone.

At this training, I didn't know anyone. The corporation housed the trainees. We were assigned rooms with two to three per home. It was one of the first times I felt like an outsider. I felt like I was being scrutinized. For one, the women all wore nice suits. I wore my best San Diego clothes. In San Diego, we wore suits mainly for customer visits, otherwise, it was business casual.

No one talked to me, even in the car going back and forth to headquarters. At dinner, there was the small talk, but I also listened to the plans for after dinner that I was not invited to. I stayed in the room reading. I hated this trip and wished that I'd never have to repeat a trip like this again!

Then I received a call that my uncle passed away. This was one of my Dad's brothers that we rarely saw. The call was on the bedroom phone so I couldn't walk outside so my roommate heard the conversation. She gave me her condolences and softened up after then. Maybe my uncle should have died a few days earlier. I'm kidding, but why did it take a death for her to soften up?

Atlanta is where our systems resided. I remember having to coordinate our order entries in the system. During quarter closes, we had problems. The East Coast was entering last-minute orders late into the night. Meanwhile the West Coast was also entering orders during the normal business hours. With too many users, the systems froze and aborted our orders. There was a lot of cursing if it aborted in the middle of a long order. Many times, we worked late, waiting for the East Coast to end their day.

The second time I went to Atlanta, Cierra and, I think, it was Liz who went with us. It was either to learn about third-party contracts or to learn accounts receivables. At about this time, we were becoming two Regions, South and West. Both regions decided that the CSR's would be enriched, meaning that we were responsible for everything from order entry to collecting invoices. That was my part because Cierra and Liz continued to be dedicated to Accounts Receivable.

On this trip I was part of the evening events. We also shopped and I took home a couple of new suits, one beige and one plum. The suits were so much nicer from Atlanta. They were wool and lined. I still have the plum one hanging in the closet. I had hoped to pass it on to my daughter, but my waist was about 25" and even my thinnest athletic nieces couldn't fit in it.

One evening we had dinner and stayed for cocktails. It was a venue that had pictures of the Beatles. Cierra asked me the name of one she pointed at. I couldn't answer her, I had no idea. I was embarrassed, and it instantly took me back to my Spelling Bee Day. They all thought I couldn't guess because I had too much to drink but it was that they had too much and didn't suspect how naïve I was and humiliated I felt. Interesting how you can feel humiliated and at the same time relieved!

During the contract lessons, I fell asleep. I could not keep my eyes open. The next few days, I switched to a seat right in front of the instructor, hoping I'd stay awake. There was no way to keep my eyes open. After class, I apologized to the teacher, telling him that it might be the difference in time that I couldn't get used to. I remember that when I was at Pima, I took a computer class and the same thing occurred. In fact, the one teaching it was my brother-in-law Phil. I'd fall asleep and somehow the lesson transferred to my brain. It amazes me how I became an expert in the tasks that I slept through!

Going back to wearing suits. As a Customer Support Rep, I needed to wear a suit more often, especially when we had to meet with customers. There was one day I dressed in the beige suit. I was wearing high heels. On the way to work, the car stalls on the freeway. I was able to get it onto the shoulder. Ralph was traveling so he wasn't of help. We didn't have cell phones, so I stood outside the car wondering what to do. At that moment, a young man comes walking down the steps from the apartment complex that was on the hill next to where I was parked. He asked if I needed help. I was desperate so I told him the car had just died on me. He opened the hood and checked a few things then pulled out the oil stick and it was bone dry.

"You know that a car needs more than gasoline!" he teased me. He then took me up to his apartment to look for a can of oil. He was gay, and his apartment confirmed it, very orderly and clean. There was a picture of him and another man. Both were very handsome. It took him a while to get the oil can, so I sat down on his couch and waited. He then cheerfully bounced up the stairs with can in one hand and an old towel in the other. We walked back down, me holding onto the rails lest I trip and fall. I always fall, that's why Mom used to point out my scars.

I had a twenty-dollar bill, but I needed lunch money, too. I didn't know how I was going to pay him. I asked if I could pay him something and he refused. I was relieved. He just told me to do someone a favor, pay it forward! He was my angel that morning. I was late but I was safe!

Around this time, I made sure my hair looked nice. I decided to get a perm. My hair was very long so it took six hours total from start to finish! I looked like the lion from the Wizard of Oz. After a few weeks it settled down and looked halfway decent. The hairdresser's shop was in Hillcrest, known as the gay community. I never got his name right, James Michael or Michael James. I always seem to travel far for hair care. He was very good and after a few months of the perm, he gave me a very nice short cut only after I had given a Dress for Success presentation.

My sister, Laurie, was working at a high school in Tucson. She was preparing students for their future. She had heard my stories of dressing nice for work and wearing suits. She asked if I would give her class a presentation on Dressing for Success. I gladly accepted and planned it for the next trip.

On the day of the presentation, I put gum in my mouth, had my hair over my face and wore loud jewelry. I was wearing a necklace, multiple bracelets, and big hoop earrings. I started with messy clothes. My shirt was untucked, and my skirt was not completely zipped. I had my suit coat hanging on a chair for easy access. I wore high heels. When I was introduced, I came walking in like I didn't know how-to walk-in heels. I asked the students what they thought of my appearance. They were very attentive. After they pointed out what didn't look good, I fixed my hair, zipped my skirt, and straightened it and finished tucking in my shirt then put my suit jacket on. I removed the necklace and all but one bracelet. I left the earrings on. I gave them a lesson on how a properly dressed employee will be seen as someone who cares just by looking at how they dress. Do they care enough to look for clean clothes for work? Or did they get up and grab whatever was on hand maybe even on the floor? My sister said they really enjoyed the presentation. I had fun and even thought of doing it again with another group but as always, there was not enough time on my schedule.

New Building
More Responsibility

*"Earning happiness means doing good and working,
not speculating and being lazy. Laziness may look
inviting, but only work gives you true satisfaction."*
—**Anne Frank**

I was becoming aware of the company's structure. Previously, I focused on the small departments I supported but never had the thought to pull up an organization chart to see how high it went and how low I was on the totem pole. Perhaps it was a good thing; otherwise, I would have been disappointed to find that I had a long way to go. I also wasn't motivated to move fast because I didn't understand any of that. My focus was to not be bored. I craved challenges and I wanted to keep my mind occupied. It also never occurred to me what in life I was trying to block. I was anxious, restless, and at the same time excited about my new way of living.

Soon after the last Atlanta trip, we joined a new division and during that same time we were moved to a new building with assigned cubicles that helped tone down the noise. The floor that was leased was split so that the Northwest and Southwest Branches were separated. They each had their own Sales Branch managers. We had one financial manager for both sides of the house. We might have had one Admin manager for both Branches, but I don't recall.

With this move, I was assigned to a new manager. I was also now an enriched Senior Support Rep, handling all parts of an order beginning with the orders, backlog management, transportation, accounts receivable, collection, etc., whereas other Regions had one support rep handling all orders and a separate group handling accounts receivable. An order began with hand-written orders from the customers since we didn't have networking systems as we have today. All orders were either faxed or mailed in. We were limited to the big systems for ordering into the plants and the headquarters administrative systems.

The orders we received were literally manually transferred to a paper order template to keep all orders consistent. The paper order contained the product number, description, quantity, and the price that the customer showed on their order. The price was 90% of a price that their Representative quoted. On top of the order, we noted whether the order would be financed or cash. If the order included software, the CSR had a system engineer configure the order and provide each code pertaining to the license and software revision number. We also shared the orders with the Maintenance Reps so that they could do the selling of the Maintenance. They carried a separate quota from the Sales Reps.

Once the order was successfully placed, we filed it in our desk drawer under the shipment date to follow up. This is what we called backlog management and was all manual. Once it shipped, we filed it again to follow up for payment. We couldn't file the order until all aspects of the processes were complete, then it went into the big metal file cabinets that we all shared.

Transportation and shipping of products were also manual. We spent hours with the shipping carriers and then hours were spent trying to get the truck to the correct customer dock. Afterwards, we had to manually track the transportation invoices and pass them on to the Transportation administrator, Hank.

Hank was an older man who always had jokes to tell. He was also the most stubborn man on our floor. He refused to learn the new systems that would eventually make his tasks so much easier. He was also very sneaky. He hid his cigarette packet in his socks so that his wife wouldn't know he was smoking (as if she couldn't smell it!!) He and his wife fostered children with physical disabilities. They were eventually too much for them to give them quality care. Hank was very sad when the final child left their home. He retired and I heard he had passed away not too long after.

With the new seating arrangements, I sat next to Luke. He was a step ahead of me. He was the Marketing Administrative Assistant. I was also beginning to receive assignments of larger accounts.

To someone who doesn't understand the life of an order, and everything involved, they wonder how we keep track of all the detail involved. I found it very satisfying to let my creativity find ways to create new processes that made the task at hand more efficient. I have always been an organized person, (I got that from my Dad) and no matter what new task I received, I always found ways to organize my notes so that I didn't have to ask my peers the same questions repeatedly. I was passionate and wanted to do more but that gets us in trouble too!

When huge systems were ordered, we were required to work closely with the Engineers and the Sales Reps. There was one time I thought I was doing a good deed, but it turned out to be bad. After being persistent with the plant, I was able to get a large system shipped and delivered to the customer before month's end, and it was also the end of the year, and the Rep didn't complain nor stopped me from pressuring the plant. This was going to pay the sales rep his commissions plus a monetary bonus for having sold a million-dollar system. The next day, early in the morning I was called into my manager's office.

"I see that we had a system ship prematurely!" I'm getting worried the more she talks.

We should never allow the shipment of a large system without going through system assurance to ensure the customer is all set up and ready to receive the machine.

"We need to report to the Branch Manager."

Thankfully, he was very understanding. I felt awful since the company had to take the expense to return the system to the plant. Although I had caused this error, this was the year that I received a very prestigious award and was sent to Orlando for a few days of entertainment with some of my peers from within the Division.

It was my first time attending a big conference. When we first arrived, we went to a ranch style buffet lunch. It was outside by a river, so it was very humid. My arthritic body could not handle the moisture, so I was very uncomfortable. The indoor meetings felt better. The meetings included motivational speakers. In the evenings we were free to do what we wished except for the dinners. They paid for all meals. They also brought in a celebrity for entertainment. On one of these trips, we had Donny Osmond!

In 1985, I began supporting the Maintenance Sales Reps. I was also more involved with invoicing and collections. One time I was sent to Rancho Cucamonga, about a two-hour drive to deliver a $14-million check. It was nerve wracking and I had thoughts someone was following me. I got used to the money as the months went by and became more experienced.

Rather than supporting many accounts, I was assigned to a few very large accounts. One of them was a large Aero Space company where my husband worked. We also had offices at one of their facilities that I worked out of. When I was assigned the large accounts, I was also paired up with Luke. He assisted the sales reps with their proposals and orders and then turned them over to me.

Luke missed work off and on. He had a drinking problem. I could smell it when he spoke to me. He wore cowboy boots and dressed western. He was very friendly with the ladies; sometimes too friendly. I tolerated him because he was nice to me and not obnoxious. One day out of the blue he asks, "What color do you like, red or black?" "Red!" I said, wondering what he was up to! That's all that was said.

Right before Christmas break, Luke showed up with a gift wrapped in pretty, shiny, red paper. He had me open it right away. In the box was a set of red satin sheets. I had no idea what to think or what to say. "Um, thank you. Very pretty!" I quickly blurted out. That's all I could think to say.

My husband looked at them and I'm sure he had the same thought I had. Since that day, I was very leery of Luke, but things got back to normal, and I started feeling sorry for him.

He left to visit his grandchildren, whom he adored. He always came back a different man. I don't know what happened during the last visit. Shortly after, our manager announced that he had passed away; he had over-dosed. This stunned the office, and it affected me much more than I expected. I often think of him and send little prayers to him and to his grandchildren whom he loved with his whole being and were probably the only thing that kept him going.

His replacement was Ben. We ended up working for some time together. He and his wife became close with many in our group. One time he invited our group to his home to treat us to "his" chicken. Ben bragged about "his" barbecued chicken! I remember that it looked like he had grilled dozens of chickens!!

One of my accounts was part of the maquiladoras. I recall it was Sony, an American company doing business in Mexico and exporting their manufactured products to the American distribution center or directly to the end user customer. With all maquiladoras, there was the headquarters and distribution centers in the U.S. and Mexico had their mini headquarters and manufactured the product that was then shipped to the U.S. So, it's the same company with business performed on both sides. Sony was one of the first maquiladoras accounts I visited. We had a few American accounts in Tijuana.

Jacob, the Sales Representative was assigned the Sony account. He invited me to join him on this call as an interpreter (if needed, most spoke English) but also to take notes. His goal was to sell them a computer system. I remember sitting in one of the offices looking at the construction. It had just been built and it looked like it was done in haste! It was poorly built. I am no expert in constructing a building, but I could see the wall paint leaked on the floor and it was not cleaned. The doors had gaps and the walls were very thin. We could hear the conversations from the office next door so I'm sure they were hearing ours. It was an interesting visit and reminded me of when I went with Uncle Bud to Hermosillo and when we visited the maquiladora companies with my class. Back then I had no idea that I was being prepared for this day.

After our meeting we stopped at a café to summarize what we learned. We must have sat for at least two hours. Jacob ordered us coffee and the cups kept getting refilled. I don't drink coffee, so don't know why I chose to this time. That night my face went numb, and I thought I was going to have a heart attack. My husband was traveling, so I worried throughout the night. I didn't see a doctor right away but when I did, he suggested I never have coffee of any sort since it is the bean I reacted to.

To have been allowed to go on this trip with the sales rep was a sign of trust. The sales rep appreciated my hard work and I know that he gave my manager good feedback. He was not the only rep that praised me. The Maintenance lead Rep also kept me busy with his projects. He would tell me I was a slice from heaven. He gifted me with a thank you gift, a beautiful crystal vase that I still use! Reps were coming to me for favors to help with sales projects. The System Engineers taught me to configure software for small systems. At least I could take that off the reps' plate and let them concentrate on the more difficult configurations.

Not Good Enough

I was about to be disappointed, and I blamed myself for not understanding the company and its management policies. It was not something I needed to understand, nor did I ever have the need to know. Is this something taught in the business class I didn't complete? Was it taught when I was just hired and slept through it? In any case, it appears that no one else had the desire for the position or they were also caught off guard, but I was the only one who reacted as I did.

Working with my peers was good. We all got along. We each had our strengths and helped each other. A new CSR transferred from another Region. She was also a Senior CSR. She was a young lady with numerous years of experience. We collaborated well. She joined some of our afterwork activities.

When the time came for a promotion to a management position, I truly thought I had a chance. I had been awarded dinners, money, trips for going above and beyond my duties. My peers sought me, and reps gave me nothing but praise. So why would I not be considered for a promotion?

One morning we were called to a central office. Everyone was gathered, and the new manager was announced. I thought I was going to faint when I heard the name, someone whom I least expected. Once the shock ran through the core of my body, I knew I had to leave the building. I went back to my desk as quietly and as quickly as possible to retrieve my purse and keys. I left the building not knowing where to go because my tears were non-stop, something very unusual for me. I rarely cry but these were tears of hurt, anger, and stupidity. Why would I think I had a chance for that position?

I found a fountain with a waterfall at a mall not too far from the office. I sat for a very long time. I remember that I could not stop crying and people stared at me and when I tried to hide my distress, I continued to sob. I was inconsolable. I was truly a hopeless case and I needed to get back to lock up my desk. One woman stopped to ask if I was okay. I just shook my head, and she tapped my shoulder and left.

I recall going back to the office, finding a few employees still in the building who looked at me with pity. A few hugged me and told me they were sorry, as if someone had died. This made me want to cry even more. It's how when a baby is on the verge of crying, but they are holding it back until you baby-talk to them and then they let it out. So, I packed it up and went to the car to finish crying.

Any hope of advancing had died. Fortunately, I got over it in one night, probably because Mom hated when we got emotional. I called her that night and as usual, she gave me her spiritual advice.

Later when I put my pride aside, I thought I understood why I wasn't considered. I didn't have the management skills, I'm guessing. Plus, I was needed for the actual tasks and this pattern continued through the rest of my career. Years later, when I remembered that when new jobs are posted, we apply for them. I don't ever remember a post for the position, so I remained wondering if this new person needed to transfer as I was transferred from Tucson to San Diego and the position was already set aside for her or I just wasn't good enough?

The next day the CFO called me into his office and gave me a little "father" talk. I heard him but I wasn't listening to anything he said. I was still hurt and holding a grudge. I wished I would have paid attention so that I didn't continue to think it was because I was a minority but that is all I could think of. I also believed that I was not good enough. I was the team lead, the "go to." It hurt more when one of the Customer Support Reps from another team came by and shared her surprise with the selected candidate.

In later years I learned that a promotion to a higher level doesn't necessarily have to be to a management position. I did congratulate the young lady who was given the position and we continued to be good friends. Once again, I kept my faith that something would come my way.

The following two years I received a prestigious award that sent me to San Francisco and the other was in San Diego which wasn't as much fun since it was in my hometown!

There was one interesting show that occurred at the San Diego event. We stayed in a hotel in Mission Bay. The hotel had many floors. Photographers gathered us and announced that they are taking us to one of the top floors. We were given an index card, each receiving parts of the lyrics of one of the Huey Lewis and the News songs. Three at a time were to hang over the balcony of the room, reading the memorized lines. Plus, we had to move around as if we were dancing to the song. I was freaking out. I am afraid of heights, but I did it.

I don't know how the photographers videoed our front sides. When it was shared at the event on a large screen, it looked amazing and professional. The song was played in the background and so it appeared that the lyrics were coming out of our mouths. They also made it look like multiple windows were used because everyone in the group appeared in the video, sometimes side by side.

The administrators were also invited to dinners at the five-star restaurants with the top salesmen. These were called the Branch

Manager awards. Then we had the Better Mouse Trap awards for sharing new ideas with the team, like refining procedures.

My manager encouraged me to put in writing the Demo and Trial procedures listing the rules of when commissions are paid. My role had nothing to do with commissions, but I had to work with the commission analysts that resided in Atlanta and with the one commission analyst in our office. I was the liaison between the reps and the Commission Analysts. I was the one who answered the reps' questions when they complained about not getting paid for their sales when it was for a Trial machine or a demo. I went with my manager's suggestions, wrote out the procedures and had a great time putting it together. It was easy enough for me, since I had the steps memorized. I received a $3,700-dollar award for submitting it and it was implemented. Plus, the procedure was used by both branches. Later, it was implemented in other Regions, and I received another $300. I bought myself a ring with a ruby and diamonds that I still wear today. These perks with my faith kept me going and climbing the ladder, one-baby step at a time.

I continued to work in a senior position. Got involved in after-work partying and felt so very much part of the sales teams. We also had softball tournaments against each other when we could, sometimes weekly or every other week. After playing we went to El Indio, a small Mexican restaurant that has since grown to a much bigger and more popular place.

One time when my parents visited, we took them to El Indio for dinner. We were sitting outside on a bench next to the restaurant door. They had huge avocado trees. Unbeknownst to me, mom had cut an avocado from a branch hanging over near her. She put it in her purse, and it wasn't until we were driving back home that we found out.

"Mira lo que me encontré! Look at what I found!"

"You found it, or did you take it?" I asked. She repeats this story to everyone.

The softball group sat outside and chitchatted until it got dark. Before departing we planned the next outing. Sometimes we met at Liz's mother's restaurant right in La Jolla. We had drinks and appetizers or sometimes a full dinner. On weekends we met at the beach and sat around a bon fire and had a late evening picnic and drinks.

There was a new guy who transferred from Florida who was young and very shy. He was to help us. My circle of friends decided to take care of him, and he loved the attention. We took him to Boll Weevil's, a hamburger joint that was very popular. They served condiments that included small yellow, spicy peppers. Cierra put a couple on his plate and didn't tell him they are spicy, and he confidently bit into one. His face turned bright red. We introduced him to good Mexican food, and we tried to introduce him to a couple of young single females. He never asked anyone out, though. He hung out with us wherever we went.

We also took him to the "Over the Line." It's a game played on Fiesta Island. It's played like baseball but with only three players on a team. The clothes the players wear is interesting, with some obscene but mostly humorous. Everyone drank all day and at night went home dehydrated! That was the only time we went.

We invited him to our home during the holidays since he couldn't afford to fly home to be with his family. He even went to aerobics classes with me so that I wouldn't go alone, being that I didn't like doing anything on my own. He gladly volunteered. To my embarrassment, someone took a picture of us during one of our aerobics classes and it was posted in a newspaper.

In later years I had the occasion to work with him in Atlanta. Within a year he developed a brain tumor and passed away shortly after. I will never forget him. He was so sweet and would do anything for us. I sent his dad the picture from aerobics and wrote stories of his short life in San Diego. I received a nice thank you note a few weeks later. He especially thanked me for the stories and said that his son mentioned our little group more than once!

Around this time, my youngest brother came to visit us. He was so excited, but the excitement left when we received the call that Tata was in his last days. We made quick reservations to return to Tucson to join the family's drive to Rayón. We made it right before he passed. I remember wearing white pants with a red top. Tata looked at me, then let out a chuckle and told me I'm pretty and that he loved me very much. I was very much surprised with his last words. I'll cherish that moment forever.

Back in San Diego, I was dealing with personalities. Some of the reps were very hard to support, especially one female rep that was demanding and very difficult to deal with. She was a very successful seller, and I must give her that, as she well deserved it. She also wore the most expensive perfume that made me want to puke when I was pregnant. She announced one day that she had received a nice offer from another company. I was so relieved when I heard the news in the office gossip. When I saw her in the restroom, I congratulated her with such enthusiasm, but it was more for me to never have to work with her again! I am sure she was successful in her new position, and I sincerely wished her well!

In my future career, I came across many more demanding and difficult employees, but I knew how to handle them and learned how to work with them. The easiest way was to find something funny about them and keep it to myself. It made it easier to deal with their pettiness.

I also coordinated our office family Holiday Party on top of my day-to-day tasks. It was for more than 200 guests. I had the responsibility of finding a Santa, caterers, decorations, and a photographer. The event was a success. I thought I was volunteering through a corporate group, but Travis, one of our Reps, took it upon himself to request I get compensated for my work and in doing so, he discovered that there were funds set aside for the Event Planner position. I didn't hesitate to accept the payment, although I would have done it for free since it was all for fun and was a great experience.

Gaining New Friends

"Laughter is not at all a bad beginning for a friendship, and it is by far the best ending for one."
—Oscar Wilde

I say, "gaining new friends" but normally work friends are just temporary. I would say they are more family away from home. We work with them all day, sometimes eat with them, and share personal stories with them. We meet outside of work hours. Yet, when we leave to pursue other interests, these friends become non-existent unless you work hard to keep the friendship. I left many behind, but if we meet somewhere years later, we can get into conversation as if we had just seen each other yesterday.

During one of our offsite classes, there were about 15 students all working for the same company and in the same field. Cierra and I were paired up into groups of five. In my group there were three administrators who handled collections and nothing else. One of them always stared at me in class and I often wondered if I had something hanging out of my mouth or nose.

One day while we were all eating lunch his friend, David, who was one of the guys in our group whispered something to him that made him very uncomfortable. David couldn't stop laughing but the guy who stared at me got up and left. The next day when David was alone, we asked what he whispered in the guy's ear. What he told him was, "Quit staring at Sylvia, she's married, and so are you!"

Later the guy who stared told David that he didn't know it was obvious and that he didn't mean anything by it. This was embarrassing to me as well and more so because the guy who stared continued to stare at me. He was odd in that his mustache was painted on or at least it looked like it was. I thought it was very peculiar.

David and one of the other guys in the group became our friends. The guy who stared did not and I never heard about him or from him again other than that he had become a manager. The rest of the group came to my 30th birthday party. David and his girlfriend gifted me with a sexy red dress. They made me try it on at the party. How embarrassing was that! Now that I think of it, what a strange gift to give at a birthday party to someone who you barely met and was not family. How odd. I didn't think so then. But I tried it on!

During this time, I was also a friend with another lady who was about five years older than I. She was single and was a workaholic. She was the Commission Analyst for both branches. We found ways to get her out. We scheduled girl nights to play cards or board games. We had wine nights, game nights, and dinner nights. We exchanged gifts during Christmas and birthdays; we spent time with her mom and her sister.

I loved this lady since she was a very big part of my nine months of pregnancy, preparing for the arrival of our daughter. She also motivated us during the big month-end closes by bringing us "anti-cranky" cookies. She was known for her baked goods. Somewhere along the years, she abruptly stopped communicating with us and to this day I have no idea why. Maybe it was the distance. I just hope she is doing well and maybe there will be a slight chance that she will appear when least expected. I miss her not for her cookies but for the laughter she brought to our circle of friends.

The Slips

"Almost nothing needs be said when you have eyes."
—*Tarjei Vesaas*

Embarrassing moments break the monotony of weeks of hard work. You get to the point when you no longer care that you make a fool out of yourself. Life goes on.

In 1989 I had already gone through five years of trying to get pregnant. I had gained weight, so I decided to get on HCG (Human Chorionic Gonadotropin) and Vitamin B+ shots. The HCG and B12 injections with a low-calorie diet (500 to 800 calories), was a fast way to lose my weight. Only two meals are allowed. I had chicken or beef with a salad. I did this for a few months and lost a few pounds and inches. One very early morning as I was walking into the lobby, the slip I was wearing started crawling down my thighs. I didn't have a free hand. I was carrying a water jug and purse and paperwork and so I didn't know what to do. Our old guard that we brought with us to the new building occupied the front desk. I always wondered how he would handle an unexpected incident! Well, I made his day. He laughed so much as I struggled. I put my things down on his desk and took the slip off right in front of him. He just shook

167

his head laughing and I laughed with him! I made him promise not to tell anyone.

Around this same time, I got on the elevator very early in the morning. When I say very early, I mean before 6 a.m. There were already a few construction workers with their tools and their work clothes. We were all stuffed in the elevator. They all stared, and I stared back. It took me a few seconds to realize one was my neighbor.

"Oh, I didn't recognize you with your clothes on," slips out of my mouth.

You know what kind of a reaction I got. I had to quickly explain that I see him in shorts and a grass hat at home while he's working in his yard and had never seen him in his work clothes. Of course, I got teased about this for some time!

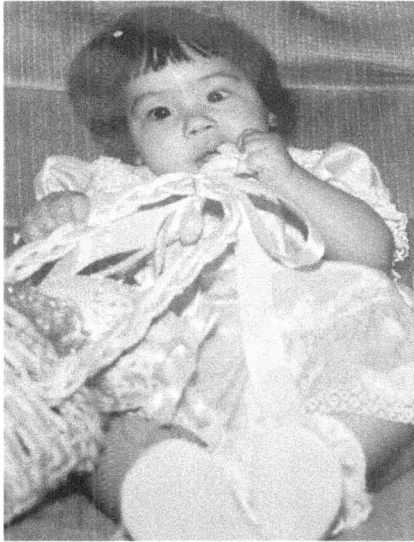

Melissa at 6 months - 1992.

Melissa shortly after we moved to Colorado – 1993.

Melissa is Born

"You're the best thing I never knew I needed."
—The Princess and the Frog

We waited so long for our only child and what a joy it was to have others with new babies to mingle with. It was also a delicate experience. She was not a computer nor a telephone. She was our human machine.

There was so much to learn, and like all new parents, we anticipated that all would be easy and that nothing would change — and then there's the realization that yesterday will never be the same.

For some, caring for a newborn is initially a difficult task; for others, it comes naturally. Having many siblings that I helped care for, it was easier for me to transition to be a new mom except for the feeding. Once Melissa got on a schedule, things became easy especially during the day while she slept.

I also became too comfortable staying at home with her. Having her close to me.

Then we are given advice, one to let her go and the other was a meeting between friends, and we were left to make decisions.

Also there, was the weight I gained. What a struggle to lose it again, taking at least 33 years to completely go back to a decent size.

In October 1990, our daughter was born at Scripps Memorial Hospital in La Jolla. She was conceived after having some endometriosis removed and taking fertility pills and I guess losing weight helped, too! It took us about six years to conceive our miracle baby. I took a year of maternity leave. The doctor who delivered her was amazing and a little selfish. The birth was induced, so I had asked Dr. Vandenburg if he could induce her on my husband's birthday, October 19th. He refused, because he had a golf tournament, so Melissa was born on the 18th.

Dr. Vandenburg sent us a Christmas card with a picture of his staff and nurses. The nurses were all dressed in black dresses, and he was sitting right in the middle in a black tuxedo. He was the coolest doctor I've ever had, even if he golfed instead of delivering our baby.

There were three other sales reps who had babies weeks apart. We met at Hotel Del Coronado to walk with babies in strollers and stopped for lunch. Everyone commented about how much Melissa slept. It is true, she slept all day but was awake all night. At night I danced around the house with her in my arms until she fell asleep. I didn't nurse her, so she was always hungry. Her cry was so strong and long that we couldn't get a bottle in her mouth until she relaxed. Mom was with me the first week and so when I couldn't deal with her during some of these nights, she took her to bed with her and Melissa slept peacefully. She must have sensed my stress.

A few weeks later, I took Melissa to the office to show her off. On the way home right when I turned to get onto the freeway, I heard a "thump", and I looked back, and Melissa was gone! The car seat had slipped off the car seat with Melissa landing face down underneath it. I had forgotten to strap her in securely. At least I had her strapped tightly in her chair. I was thankful she was not hurt.

Her 1st birthday was with family. It was a small party since she was too small to enjoy it. On her 2nd, it was a much bigger birthday party held at the Santee Lakes, close to our home. All the babies and moms were invited. We had barbacoa (spiced meat), rice, and beans. We wanted to share the Mexican food with our friends. We also had a cake and a piñata and party favors.

It was a good time, but I remember that Melissa was so uncomfortable in the outfit I put her in. I wanted her to look stylish. It was a one-piece pant set made from sweatshirt material. The design was in fall colors. Her birthday was in October, but it was still very warm. This is also when all the new fall colors are popping out at the stores, so I thought it was perfect. Nope, that was not a good idea.

Our baby group continued until we all began going back to work. It was time to find a babysitter. I was so nervous to leave her with strangers. The doctor at one time scolded me, "If you don't let go, Melissa won't know what to do without you if something serious happens to you."

That scared me, so I started the search for someone I could trust. Someone recommended Suzette, as she was already licensed and had a couple toddlers including her son and daughter. Melissa was a perfect fit. We gave it a try for a couple of days during the week about two months before I went back to work. Melissa had a blast and never missed us. We loved Suzette.

While she was at Suzette's, I went shopping for clothes since I had not lost the weight I had gained. It was a sad experience. I decided to go to the Old Navy that had just opened by our house. It was all young, rude clerks. I had a few clothes I wanted to try on, so I stood in line at the dressing room. The clerks allowed the teen-agers behind me in, and I kept wondering why they were overlooking me. I stood a little longer and again someone else was let in, while I grew impatient and angry. Finally, I spoke up and the young girl said, "Oh," and let me in next.

I heard her and the other clerk laughing at me. They were so proud of being mean. I was the only Hispanic and a big lady so the only thing I could come to was that they didn't like people like me.

I also went for big grocery shopping, buying food for lunch. I was in the garage unloading groceries and left the garage door open. I was just setting a bag on the counter when I hear a knock. Instead of opening the garage door, I went through the front door.

"How did you get out?" screamed the mail lady who is in the garage waiting for me to open the door.

"Through the front door," I said.

"There's a rattle snake curled up right in front of the door!" she said, and I jumped right on top of her screaming. Oh my gosh, we laughed so hard. The darn snake was still there! I don't recall what happened to it. I was just glad Melissa wasn't home or she would have followed me out.

Even after going back to work the moms and babies continued to meet but this time, we included the dads. During one outing, when not all the moms were present, we were told that the moms had discussed Melissa sleeping with us. They suggested it was not healthy and we needed to make sure she slept in her crib. I'm listening, not understanding. Maybe it is just our upbringing, but we know many parents who allow their kids to sleep with them occasionally. Melissa was brought to our bed in the middle of the night when she was fussing. To make a point, Melissa grew up just fine.

It's just like some suggest you don't hold your baby too much, for whatever reason. We held her when we wanted to and for as long as we wanted to, and she grew up just fine. Maybe I over-did it because in my case, we weren't held enough.

The Announcement – Layoff

It's not how hard you can hit; it's how hard you can get hit and keep moving forward.
—Sylvester Stallone

During my leave, the company made an announcement that the administration department was moving to Phoenix. We were allowed to temporarily stay until all work was moved to Phoenix. I worked for the next year and a half collecting accounts receivable and continued supporting the Maintenance Reps. I also helped with a business partner project. It was new to me. I was hoping it wouldn't be assigned to me, but it turned out to be a blessing for my future.

Business Partner work is another line of work. Business Partners are contracted and are aligned with Sales Reps. There are also contracts involved, indicating how the Business Partner will be compensated. This meant learning new contracts. There are incentives given to the Business Partner, such as rebates. I learned that the Reps could get very creative, too!

174

Finally, it all ended for us in San Diego, because in 1993, my husband was laid off. What a stressful period this became with both of us losing our jobs. Fortunately, my husband's company allowed him to work out of Hammond, Louisiana until he found work. I had to resign, knowing there was no chance of my husband finding work in Phoenix where most of my peers ended up.

We packed up our home as much as we could. Our house was put up for sale. Separately, we packed all that we needed to stay in a hotel for four weeks if it took that long for my husband to find employment. Our temporary home was at a hotel in Covington, Louisiana. My husband commuted to Hammond. Melissa and I lived in the hotel for those weeks. I had flash cards I used to teach her basic words. We walked to Shoney's for breakfast every morning after Dad left to work. Her favorite breakfast was the small white powdered donut holes. It was hard getting her to eat something nutritious, but she had better lunches and dinners, so I didn't care. I knew this wasn't going to be permanent.

We drove to New Orleans on weekends and walked the streets. It got gross after we began seeing urine stains on the walls, especially on Bourbon Street. Melissa was in her stroller, so she was getting the dirtiest view where the urine accumulated.

One day we wanted to visit the church and when we got to the front to go up the stairs, there was a man with long, dirty, stringy hair, wearing dirty pants, a tank top with huge balloons as breasts. He was filthy and looked ridiculous. Suddenly, I heard a little voice. "Look, there's a chu chu man!" Melissa was saying with excitement. "Chu chu" to her were the breasts. We decided to stick to the smaller town, Hammond, where my husband was working at.

My husband was called in for an interview in Boulder, Colorado. He left us for two days for the interview and was offered the job. What a relief!

We drove back to San Diego, from Covington, to finish packing for our move to Colorado. We had to drive through Texas and New Mexico. Ralph was tired, so I tried driving but got lost getting on one of the freeways in Texas. A cop pulled me over. "I'm sorry, I was confused, I didn't know where I was going!" I volunteered before he even says anything. "Okay, just be careful!" and I was freed with no citation, again!

Ralph was livid but was wishing I'd get a ticket. I never get tickets as many times as I've been stopped.

On our drive, we also stopped in Tucson to visit our families. We talked my dad into helping us with our move. He and one of my brothers agreed to help. I made Dad feel useful and so he was happy.

The people who bought our house didn't like the vines growing on the wall leading to the house's entry so that was Dad's first job to do. We were only at the house for a week. Dad went back home, and we waited for the moving vans. We were fortunate that the new company paid for the move to Boulder, Colorado.

When we made the move to Colorado, it was exciting to be in a new place. We were put up in a small apartment in Boulder. The tenant below us met us right away. She occasionally brought her granddaughter to play with Melissa. I got into crafting with her until we bought our new home.

Waiting for the construction on our home to be finished was getting me antsy. I called the construction office every other day. We were finally given the date for the inspection. All was good and we made our move. We had two semi-trucks filled with our furniture and one also included Ralph's old Chevy truck that he used to haul trash and the one he'll be buried in. That's what I tell him! The neighbors, I am sure, were looking out their windows. The loads didn't arrive until the day after we moved in. We slept in front of the fireplace on blankets the first night. Ralph had to go present himself at work, so I was left to handle the rest of the move.

I became a sad, stay-at-home mom. I was already depressed because I couldn't conceive another child. I wanted Melissa to have a sibling but month after month of fertility pills brought only more depression. I was also mourning the loss of my work. I had worked for so many years and I didn't know how to be anyone else. I was lonely but wasn't excited to meet neighbors.

When I saw a little girl Melissa's age, I knew I had to go introduce myself. Melissa needed friends more than I did.

"Hi! Are you the one calling the construction workers?"

I was so embarrassed that they were talking to our neighbors about my persistence!

Kathy welcomed us and Melissa and Laurel became friends.

Melissa was only three going on four when we moved to our house in Berthoud. She was not completely potty trained, and I was worried, so I took her to the doctor. The doctor explained that because we had been unstable, it was affecting her routine. Within a month, everything was fine!

There was still one thing that we needed to wean her from. As a baby she sucked her thumb, holding the end of a blanket. She called it "Mikie." We don't know why but that is what she called it. "I want my Mikie!" she would say, and we'd hand her the blanket!

She had already stopped sucking her thumb, but she still needed Mikie to fall asleep with or when needing comfort. One time when she was misbehaving, we told her we would give Mikie to Laurel's dog. She hands us the Mikie! She didn't care!

When she went to kindergarten, she carried a piece of Mikie in her backpack and pulled it out when they had nap time, although she never slept and instead played tricks on the kids by hiding their shoes.

There was an older girl across the street that Melissa loved. They played together unless the other older friends showed up. One day, the girl made plans for the next day. She told Melissa they would play spies. Melissa prepared for the day. She put her spy toys in a small backpack. She also picked out the clothes to wear. She waited by the window, looking for her friend to come out. When she did, she was riding bikes with her friends. My heart hurt for Melissa. She sat at a chair, Mikie in hand, and watched a kid's video. It hurt more because she didn't cry and make a fuss over it. I saw the hurt and disappointment written all over her face. I explained that she must have forgotten and that those were her first friends. I also told her that Laurel was her age.

I knew I had to work, or I would go insane. I had to go for counseling.

"Why do you need a second child?" the counselor asked. I explained wanting a sibling for Melissa and how my siblings had more than one.

"Be happy with the one you have or adopt one."

Then I talked about not working and missing it. Again, the questions,

"So why can't you work?"

"I'm afraid to leave Melissa with strangers!" was my response.

I was convinced that there are many good day-care centers and even home care.

I left pondering all the information. I worried that Melissa wouldn't be accepted because she was different. A small Hispanic with dark hair and tan skin.

I began looking through the newspaper and there it was. A post from the corporation I had just resigned from, looking for someone with my skills. I sent my resume on a Saturday. On Monday afternoon I get the call to set the interview date and time. Things were moving fast. They told me the office was business casual and no need to worry about what I wore.

I look for my best "business casual" clothes. I went in for my interview on Tuesday. I interviewed with three managers, one after the other. I answered all their questions. I was not stressed and very confident for once! That same afternoon, I received a call with an offer. They explained that they could start me with a 10% raise from my previous base pay but that I would be exempt. That meant there would be no more overtime. Working overtime in San Diego gave me an unheard-of yearly salary for this type of position. The new exempt salary was going to be a decrease.

Finding childcare was hard and emotional. We finally opted for a daycare close to where we both worked. We paid weekly. When I picked Melissa up, she was by herself while the other children played together. I tried to encourage her to join the others, but she didn't really understand. The caregivers didn't try hard enough to have the other kids include her.

First Experience
In Colorado

"Ignore the people who talk about you behind your back. That's exactly where they belong."
—Jerose

When I find myself the target of hate, I bring out my home-grown armor to use as a shield against false accusations from jealous and insecure people and on top of that from those who discriminate. I had never been targeted as much as I was in Colorado.

My armor was the lessons from Mom and Dad and from the faith instilled in us. Don't fight back, pray, and be nice. These three lessons have rescued me from hurting someone or myself.

I happily got back into my comfort zone, working. Because of my prior experience, I was more cautious this time, or at least I thought I was. I was hired to implement a unique process. Then I was asked to be the team lead and that angered some of my peers. One morning I overheard an angry employee calling a manager horrible negative racial words that I won't repeat. The words shocked and hurt me, as if they were directed at me.

My unhappiness grew and I couldn't quite explain to my manager why I was so unhappy. I kept most of it to myself. Fortunately, I didn't stay long in the team lead position because I was needed in a different department supporting the Business Partner Reps. My main responsibility was to manage the Business Partner contracts and calculate rebates. I was required to monitor the contracts and ensure that the Business Partners adhered to them. Sometimes the Business Partner internal sales reps tried to go around the contract, offering the customers lower prices or giving away services.

During this position, I was also asked to be the lead of a new system. I was involved with writing a document of the design and process and performing tests. To write the steps, I needed to understand the flow and ensure the results were accurate. The Business Partners Reps were allowed to select a handful of Business Partners to test the system.

While going through the system tests, the man who was the liaison between me and the business partners had asked me to keep count of how many orders were placed, since it was the first week to test the new system. Oscar had gone home earlier in the day, so I left him a voicemail with the new count. Later in the afternoon, I listened to my voicemail and listened to one from Oscar who was calling to thank me for the count. Mr. Oscar didn't hang up and all I heard was him telling someone who was at the pool, "Oh, it's that Mexican… I don't care for her…" and I couldn't listen to the rest. I hung up the phone and put my head down, devastated, and humiliated. My team lead was sitting across from me. She came over and all I could say was that Oscar left me a voicemail that I think she should listen to. I replayed it for her and then she forwarded it to his manager. My immediate manager was on vacation, so it was sent to his backup who then sent it to our director. Well, the director was just as bad as Oscar. When I got called into his office, he explained that he knew what all had happened. I told him everything was fine, and that Oscar had already talked to me. He had apologized and admitted he had been drinking. I know that he hated to be told about the rules and that was one of the biggest reasons he didn't like me. For the racial slurs, there is no excuse.

"That's what you people all say." He emphasized the word "you." I would never forget those words. I got up and told the director I didn't need his help and left.

This is when my husband and I started seeing more racism in Colorado than we had ever experienced in California and Arizona. For example, when my husband visited with his co-workers and if one of them was doing landscaping and was looking for help, someone in the group would say, "Why don't you hire one of those Mexicans? They're cheap labor." (I also experienced this from an executive in one of our development meetings much later.)

My husband sat back wondering what race they thought he was, with them speaking so freely in front of him.

Another time, I was buying groceries at King Sooper's after work. It was the week of Cinco de Mayo. I was at the checkout waiting for my turn. Across the way, there was a male cashier screaming for the Mexicans to go home to celebrate in their own country. I was so offended by this and embarrassed at the same time. No one said anything to this young man, but I took note of his appearance and once at home I wrote a letter to the manager. The funny thing about all this is that Cinco de Mayo is an American-started holiday that goes as far back as the late 1800's. It's not celebrated in Mexico. I never received a response, but hope he was talked to.

I was also stressing about Melissa playing by herself. A couple of days later, I find Melissa has finally found a friend. She became so fond with one bald girl who had leukemia. That little girl was also an outcast, so Melissa and she became friends until the little girl stopped going. I couldn't bear to see Melissa excluded any longer, so I looked around Berthoud and was recommended to a young mother who cared for children and her toddler. She was like another Suzette! Even though Melissa was further from us, we felt confident that she was in good hands.

181

I did all I could through the testing of the system. A few of us who were involved were taken to a fancy lunch. On the way out as we walked through one of the hallways, one of the senior ladies who worked in the office for many years called me into her office. She proceeded to tell me about the experience I was about to have, as if I were born yesterday and had never eaten at a fancy restaurant.

"You will be served a very small portion of food set in the middle of a large plate surrounded by decorative sauce. You need to eat very slowly," she said as she proceeded to demonstrate with her hands.

I stood staring in disbelief. She assumed that because I was of a different color and age, I didn't have class or manners. She was not a mean person and we worked well together. I am sure she had good intentions, but I was insulted.

**Dinner in Washington, DC, at a Welding Convention.
(We know how to eat in public.)**

Resignation

*"I promise you nothing is as chaotic as it seems.
Nothing is worth your health. Nothing is worth
poisoning yourself into stress, anxiety, and fear."*
—*Peter Maraboli*

By September, I was very down, very troubled. On top of work, I had a daughter who was entering kindergarten. I disliked all the people who took advantage of me, and I started to feel anger, resentment, and depression. This is not who I am, and I didn't like feeling this way.

It was one day when I was driving home that I almost did the unexpected. There is a freeway that goes both ways, but it is divided and to get from one to the other they are separated with stop signs. This day, I thought I would just close my eyes and ignore the stop signs. During the thought, I saw Melissa flash before me.

I realized I was at my lowest and decided to write HR a long letter with my resignation. The HR director asked that I reconsider and instead to take three weeks off. I remember very well telling him that if he were in my shoes, he wouldn't stay for a minute, and it wasn't worth any amount of money. He signed my exit papers and told me I was always welcomed back.

I was so stressed that it made me sick to my stomach just thinking of looking for work. I applied at a shipping company that needed a Spanish speaker. I was offered the position on the spot. I looked at the woman and told her that I didn't feel I was ready to go back to work and that I was sorry for having wasted her time. She was so kind. She came to my side of the desk and explained that she too had left a corporate position not very long ago and understood exactly how I felt. She asked me to think about it and get back to her if I changed my mind. I never did.

Instead, I began helping Melissa's kindergarten teacher and it was the best therapy I could have had. There were about four moms who alternated. We did crafts with the kids and helped them with their lunches while the teacher focused on a student needing extra help.

We became close with the teacher. The teacher heard that Mom was a seamstress, so she had me take measurements and mailed Mom the fabric and pattern. A nice denim jumper neatly sewn by Mom was returned within a couple of weeks. Mrs. Tinius wore that jumper for a long time!

A surprise I had for Mrs. Tinius for the kindergarten graduation was a photo album of all her students. At lunch and after school, I was busy taking pictures and asking questions to have something to add underneath the student's pictures. The day of the kindergarten graduation came, and we presented Mrs. Tinius with the album. I started a trend. She loved it and had her future mom's make her an album each year she taught.

It was also at kindergarten that I met my friend, Danica. Her daughter, Elizabeth, was in Melissa's class. Danica worked so I saw her on occasion. I had not formally met her. I began knowing more about her when we started having birthday parties for our girls.

"You thought I was a bad mother," she told me one day. That's because the kids lined up next to their rooms waiting for the bell to ring to be walked into their classrooms. On one of these mornings, it was very cold. Elizabeth wasn't wearing a jacket, so I stood close to her to shield her from the cold. Anyway, the situation was that Elizabeth refused to wear a jacket that morning and to teach her a lesson, her mom let her have her way.

Elizabeth also gave me her personal life's detail, including everything about her mom's new friend. Danica was divorced and living with her future husband and soon I learned all about her family from Elizabeth.

I was also teased for burning Elizabeth's forehead, as if I did it on purpose. It was at one of the birthday parties, and all the girls decided I should style their hair. Elizabeth wanted hers curled and the curling iron slipped and burned her forehead. It was a tiny burn! Another time, I took her to a school swimming party with Melissa. Melissa is dark so I didn't worry about sun block, although I should have! Elizabeth's skin is very light, and I didn't think of sun block for her either. Well, she burned, and I felt bad. Danica understood but continued to tease me about burning her child! We became very close friends with Danica and her husband Bunker, to this day.

Danica and I also spent a weekend in Estes Park to get away from our stressful jobs. It was in October, right before our husbands hunted. We stayed in cabins or a hotel; I don't recall, but it did have an attached restaurant that was also used as a wedding venue. We had dinner and two bottles of wine. We were at the restaurant for a good three hours if not longer. We laughed all night especially about our husbands' hunting lists. They created a list of things to take hunting and preceding the item with a drawn little square for checking the items as they bought or packed them. We pretended we had the list in front of us and we'd check it with a finger, and we would laugh! I don't know why we thought that was hilarious. I guess wine makes everything funny!

Around the 2nd year is when I began to see discrimination in Melissa's class. I was at the school helping, it was during a break or recess and the kids paired up with their friends as they walked out the door. I saw Melissa joining a group of girls but was pushed aside. Melissa was obviously hurt and walked alone.

185

Melissa had no idea what had just happened. I wish I knew what went through her mind.

She saw another boy in her class who was also Hispanic sitting on a log by himself. Melissa spotted him and went and sat next to him. Again, my heart hurt for Melissa and the little boy! The boy's mom later told me that her son went home that day and happily said that Melissa was his new friend. How can such young kids know about discrimination? They may feel drawn to children of their own color but not to intentionally discriminate. It wasn't like this after this incident.

Melissa ended up with many friends; even to this day, she is seen with different groups. The older lake friends (they are in their 40's), the country dancing friends, the concert-going friends and the list goes on. And she tells me she gets numerous compliments about her skin and is asked if she goes to a tanning booth. After hearing this often, her boyfriend, answers for her, "She's Hispanic and it's her natural color."

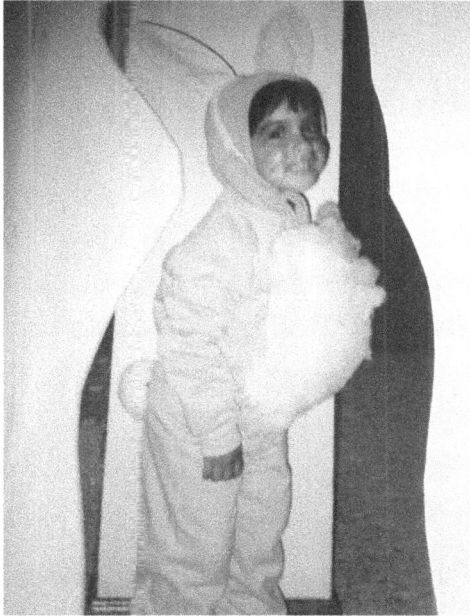

Melissa loved to dress up for Halloween.

...and she continues with the costumes, here with her boyfriend.

Employment at the City

"When he worked, he really worked.
But when he played, he really played."
—Dr. Seuss

After a year of being unemployed, I worked at one of the Colorado city offices for a year. It was a good experience with very nice people. I worked for the Planning Manager and the Planners that reported to the Planning Manager. It was a receptionist position. I was basically a very low-level secretary, separating the Planners' mail and putting City manager packets together for their weekly meetings and other duties as needed. We had corporations looking to buy land to bring new business and everything else a planning department offers. So, I was also the first contact either in person or by telephone.

Working here was like working at Pima College. It brought back memories. The departments are small, and everyone works hard but they also like to have fun.

A group of Japanese businessmen came for a meeting with the Planning Manager. I welcomed them and made small conversation while they waited. One of them reminded me of my dad. No sooner did I have the thought when he bent down and told me I could be his daughter. I chuckled and told him I had the same thought!

I took minutes at the Landmark and Historical Society meetings held once a month in the evening after work. The organization's goal was to protect old, abandoned buildings from being demolished. I also had the opportunity to see pictures of a ghost. The picture was passed around and the members inspected it as if it were no big deal!

During these nights, my hands were beginning to hurt. The arthritis pains had gone away but they were coming back quickly. It might have been the stress. Toward the last few meetings, I felt like my fingertips were being shocked, so I was so glad when they were over.

The only Halloween I experienced at the city was fun. The Planning manager asked me to bring Melissa's kindergarten class into the city's facility to Trick or Treat. The staff brought baskets of candy to put into the kids' bags. They looked so cute in their costumes, and it was fun to see Melissa having fun!

In the afternoon, a woman walked in wearing a costume. No one could figure out who she was. It was creepy, as she stared at us. She helped herself into our area and walked to each office and got close to us and stared into our eyes. Finally, one employee recognized her blue eyes and gave her away. She was from another City department. I didn't know her, personally, but I had seen her in passing.

Every Friday we had a potluck or baked goods. Then there was a Chili contest that I surprisingly won. Another time I catered food for a Holiday luncheon. During Christmas break they were invited to my home. I made a big lunch to share with them. I must have had 15 employees come and go at different times since they couldn't leave the offices unattended.

We also played. One time the Recreational director was on a two-week vacation, his friend asked me to bring in a frozen trout. He knew my husband and I fished and so assumed I might have a fish in the freezer. He wouldn't tell me why he wanted it, so I brought it in. That day at lunch he asked me to stay with him because I was going to help him tape the fish under his friend's desk. We cut the fish in half and secured it in a couple of places.

When his friend returned, he was furious with the smell and more so when he discovered where it was coming from. When my friend went on vacation a dirty trick was played on him and these pranks continued with each other when least expected.

There was a huge conference room right to the left of my office space. The wall was a window, leaving the room exposed. The Planning Director wanted a curtain, or blinds added for more privacy. I was given the honor to find something. It was fun to go through catalogs and choosing a few to present to the management and let them choose. They chose a couple and assigned me to make the final choice. I forgot what I chose but the curtains that hang over that big window are what I selected. There, I finally got my Interior Designing thrill for a quick second!

It was one of the friendliest environments, but the work was monotonous. I like being busy. I like immersing myself into the task at hand more so when it is challenging. In a way it was good that it was slow because that was the year that my Rheumatoid Arthritis came back after having been in remission for a few years.

When the doctor asked what line of business I was in, I explained and included the many hours I was putting in at my previous jobs. He was in shock. He said that even eight hours was too much for a person suffering RA. The doctor was right. Unless you have experienced arthritis pain, you have no idea how bad the pain could be. The scary part is when big joints are affected. There were times when my husband had to pull the seatbelt over me because my shoulders were in so much pain and I couldn't move them. Then he had to help me dress. All this went on until the new medication kicked in. And the snow and cold didn't help. I walked around in a smiley mask, keeping the pain inside.

When the corporation called me back, the management at the City didn't blame me. They knew where I came from and what my prior tasks entailed and knew I was bored. They gave me a going-away lunch and gifted me with a nice jacket with the City logo. That night when most had left for the day, I placed a Beanie

Baby on everyone's desk. When I bought them, I made sure to match them to their personality. It was sad to leave this group. I had become attached to the Planning manager and his staff.

One day when I was traveling to Boulder, I stopped at a Starbucks in Longmont. It was early when everyone was grabbing their cup of coffee to take into their office. The Planning manager I had worked for walked in, passing by me, and quickly backed up and stood there with his arms stretched out,

"What a treat!" We hugged and chatted briefly. It was such a good feeling. I had not seen him for a couple of years.

Rehired and Going Back Home

"It is in your moments of decision
that your destiny is shaped."
—Tony Robbins

The big corporation managers call me back. I accept only to find myself in a new environment involving new tasks and responsibilities.

Training by a man soon to retire. Grasping what I can in the short time before he leaves.

Facing a hysterectomy and coming back to a new manager and learning my future fate with new challenges and projects.

New place but same issues. Trying to fit in.

Then we face another move. This time it is back home, to Tucson and celebrating our exit from Colorado.

Finding a school for Melissa and trying to make family time.

Learning to adjust working remotely from Tucson and traveling to Boulder, to train others.

Learning new assignments and experiencing a string of new managers. Each one holding me back from moving to new positions.

Going through excruciating self-training and being called a squeaky wheel.

Haphazardly trained and yet being asked to train the world.

Painful closes, personal losses, and sorrow.

Facing drama from a manager but not mine.

Celebrating a milestone.

Joining a writer's group for an escape from work but find it intimidating. I'm still dealing with self-doubts and low self-esteem.

Experiencing our first visit to the theatre.

Dealing with a mom going through depression.

Traveling for joy.

Experiences with the final manager and the announcer of the layoff.

Post layoff experiences and immersing in personal activities including leading a casino fundraiser.

Commission Position

"The spectacles of experience; through them you will see more clearly a second time."
—Henrik Ibsen

At exactly my first-year anniversary at the City, I went back to the corporation. The lady who was working the commission desk was moving on to another position and so I was called to see if I would take her place. I was skeptical. To make me feel comfortable, HR ensured me that the main person who had caused most of my anxiety was no longer going to manage people. It was the director of sales who pushed that I accepted coming back and I was rehired, once again, with seniority!

At first, I was not comfortable with my decision. The commissions involved calculations and that was my biggest concern. I knew they were calculated on corporate systems and my responsibility was to ensure the calculation results were accurate. A lot had to do with the billing and when to release the sales. I knew I had a strong background and so I began to feel a little more confident, so I gladly accepted the position.

One of the persons who recommended me for this position was Josephine from San Diego and another lady I worked with before. Who would have thought when we were in San Diego that this lady would be in another part of the country referring me to a position, I knew very little of! I continued to work with her and the other Commission Analysts until she moved on to a new position outside of Colorado. That was a promotion for her.

The first seating arrangement was in an office in one of the aisles that was named the "estrogen" aisle, because all the women were menopausal. I think they just made it up! Soon after, Josephine and the other lady left and there were two new hires, one a transfer. We were moved to an enclosed office. We all got along just great!

One day we were all facing each other, conducting a meeting. Suddenly, a pencil lands on my cheek close to my eye. One of the quiet analysts was playing with her pencil, when it got loose! She was so embarrassed. You wouldn't have expected this from her.

I am now trained as a Commission Analyst, with Customer Support background. I also have the advantage of understanding Maintenance, Software and Services contracts from San Diego.

On the weekend I did the regular grocery shopping early on Saturday mornings. This time it felt like déjà vu, preparing for work lunches and ready with dinner ingredients just like I did when I began the very first position before I resigned. This time, though, an incident occurred.

On my way back from shopping, I was followed by a Sheriff right into our driveway. Our van had just been serviced and it was a beautiful day. When the sheriff walked to my car, I could see my husband peeking out of the kitchen window and Melissa playing outside with her friend. I'm more than embarrassed. The sheriff looks in my car and comments, "It must be time for lunch!" he says, and follows with, "Why do you think I followed you?" "For speeding? I didn't notice I was speeding, it just felt good to drive in a car that was just serviced, and I was enjoying the day." He mentioned he wasn't going to give me a citation because he saves those for the crazy reckless drivers. Then he tells me to go on in and make lunch for my family. Meanwhile, my husband is praying I get a ticket.

Back to work! I was excited and thankful for this new opportunity. I went back with renewed faith. I get into my old self, always looking for more work and more challenges. I have never liked sitting idle. Our mom trained us well!

"Tiempo perdido hasta los ángeles lloran!" Even the angels cry for the time wasted.

I had extra time to help the Customer Support Representatives (CSRs) when they got behind. I was given all the backlog and billing "to help" the CSR group. Yes, I liked to keep busy but more than anything I wanted to fit in. I soon learned that I didn't. The CSRs made happy hour plans and didn't invite me. I was left as the fool completing their work. I wish I had been braver, to have left the work, gone home to my family, and let whatever happened for the next morning.

There was one young lady who eventually warmed up to me. She asked if I could teach her how to make tortillas. I had her over a couple of times and then she left the company to raise her two children. The next time I saw her was at a Brownie's camp. It was good to see her, and I know that she will be successful in whatever she decides to do once her children are grown and in school. I looked for her once when we were looking to hire but, unfortunately, I never found her.

Excruciating Lessons

*"Being a woman is a terribly difficult task, since it
consists principally in dealing with men."*
—Joseph Conrad

For the next year, I worked with two of the senior persons.
Dennis was due to retire and so was asked to train me on a
new task that completed the commission process. He wasn't very
patient and when he knew he had gone too far he apologized
and told me it was the German in him. He also regularly told
me about his relatives who lived in Mexico as if to let me know
he wasn't a racist. (This is something I often encounter.) I just
roll my eyes.

I respected this man, and I knew that I had a lot to learn from
him since I was taking over most of his position and something
I wanted to accomplish this time without someone else taking
it away. I needed to understand it well. Part of the problem was
that I could do more for the reps than he could because I knew
the order cycle and that helped with the new task that he was
teaching me. I constantly told myself to let it go because I knew
that as soon as he left the company, I would have the freedom

to adjust as I pleased. I was just getting anxious to experience this position that included all aspects of sales and commissions.

He used to tease that he wouldn't retire, and we'd have him in a wheelchair, feeding him with a straw. He was also a whistler and that drove me nuts. I don't know what it is about these men that like to whistle on the job. I had a couple more encounters in two other positions.

Thank God for Ruben. He always came to my rescue at the right moment, right after Dennis left for the evening. He smoothed things over and the next day we were a happy little family once again. I can't say Dennis was evil because he wasn't, and I really liked him. I loved listening to his personal stories. He was kind to me when it wasn't work related. It was later that I understood why he was so demanding and sometimes fierce when training me. After all, he was leaving behind a position he held for many years and was leaving good friends behind and so I think he was having problems with detachment.

New Manager –
New Challenges

*"Success is no accident. It is hard work, perseverance,
learning, studying, sacrifice, and most of all, love of
what you are doing or learning to do."*
—Pele

In February of 2001 at 45 years of age, I had a hysterectomy and was out of work for seven paid weeks, unheard of now. When I returned to work, I found myself with a new manager, Peter. When I was introduced to him, his first words were that he was told I was shy and to be easy on me. I do tend to be shy for the first two weeks in any new environment, thereafter, people are wondering what happened to that shy lady!

When I returned, the timing was right when my yearly appraisal was due. I was consistently earning high performance appraisals so when Peter rated me a three, I marched right into his office and asked why he rated me so low.

"Because you were gone for seven weeks," he replied.

"You are appraising me for 2000, not 2001," I argued.

He agreed and had discussions with my previous two managers. Dennis was my team lead, but I also reported to two previous Directors of Sales. So, between both managers my appraisal was adjusted to coincide with the year worked.

My position was to support the Region Managers. I was to work directly with the Business Analysts from each Region. We had the West, Central and East Regions. I was the liaison between the Sales Reps and Accounts Receivable, tracking orders, invoices, and proactively reviewing customer numbers to ensure revenue flowed to the correct territories. I also served as the consultant to the Latin America and Canada Region Business Analysts and the sales teams.

At this time, we were introduced to a new Financial System (FMS). My additional responsibility was the liaison between corporate staff, sales managers, and executives in the training of the new commissions system.

I continued to learn from Dennis and because of the hours I was working, I lost a friend from the city. She was hurt that I didn't have time for her to go to lunch or meet after work. I couldn't, no matter how much I tried. My focus was to spend as much time with Dennis because I had no choice but to learn his duties. It hurt to have lost this friendship and I know that along the way I lost others. I just couldn't keep up with social events with all the overtime I was spending trying to learn my new responsibilities on top of performing my regular daily tasks and trying to have a family life. So, I apologize to all my friends whom I loved dearly and still think about.

For Dennis's retirement, I asked his wife to find photos of him and his friends that he worked with or had worked with in prior years. With those pictures I created an album and presented it to him at his retirement party. He was very touched. He later mentioned that he pulled it out to share with his visitors. We kept in touch for some time. I didn't hear from him after we moved to Tucson.

The same day that my husband found my "Personal" folder, there was a card from Dennis. He had thanked me for the album and said it was the best gift he had ever received in all the years he worked at this corporation. He even opened his home to us that was near one of the big lakes in Colorado.

"Come visit us, we have plenty of room!" We never saw or heard from him again.

After Dennis was gone, we saw more of Peter. I was mixed in a group of Financial Analysts. I was the odd ball and the only female.

On the first day that we met as a group, Noah, one of the new and younger Financial Analysts and I were the first ones in the conference room.

"Have you eaten a Chipotle burrito?" he asks me randomly.

"Yes, why?" I ask.

He begins to explain how when he ate a whole one, it went from his throat to his stomach and just sat there! It was that big! He puts one hand under his chin and the other on his belly. I got into my non-stop laughter, and it made him laugh even more. Peter walks in wondering what we are laughing at. This time he's asking Noah what is so funny and glad it wasn't me he asked like the nun did back in grade school. Peter was cool and chuckled when we could finally explain.

During our first meeting, Peter talked a lot about education and going to a university and degrees. He was going around the room asking where the analysts graduated from. I immediately tensed up because I didn't want to reveal that I didn't attend one. It was almost as if he knew and moved on to another subject.

Tucson Move

*"Once you'd resolve to go,
there was nothing to it at all."*
—Jeannette Walls

In that same year in May 2001, we found out that my husband would interview at a large company in Tucson. I worried sick that if we had to move, I would lose a job that I had worked so hard to learn. At that time, Peter was a little skeptical about my potential. I was afraid to ask if I could work from Tucson. At this time, remote work was not yet popular. He didn't know my work ethic, so he had to consult with upper management.

My husband was made an offer that he accepted, and we made the move in September 2001. In fact, we moved the day after 9/11. Peter advised me that I could take my work with me! This was the best gift ever!

My husband's company threw him a going-away party at a local brewery. Mine was also at the same place the same night. It turned out to be a very crazy exit from this point of my career! We toasted and we toasted and had fun and I know I had a little too much, but I deserved to toast to all the past trials and a toast to Peter for convincing the company that my work was doable remotely! I also remember that he wrote in my card something about being his golden child. I knew I had won him over and that we could work just fine from a distance.

One of my co-workers kept buying me drinks and she was drinking right along with me so at the end I know she was feeling just as I was. My friends, Danica and Bunker also came. Bunker was with Ralph and his co-workers and Danica was with me and my co-workers. Julie was one of them. She is the one I blame for what happened. We were at the bar saying good-bye, then she tells the bartender that I'm leaving and that I should have one more shot. He gives me one at no charge. I couldn't hold one swallow before I had to run to the restroom. Danica was with me. We pass by an older woman who says, "Is she going to be all right?"

"Yes, she's fine, she does this all the time!" I elbowed Danica and we moved on.

I was a happy lady that night. I remember getting on a motor-cycle with one of my husband's co-workers who gave me a tour of the city. Normally I would have been afraid to even sit on it since the day Laurie and I crashed into the mesquite tree at Uncle Bud's land, but I didn't care that night. It was a good time and nice to be with friends and co-workers. Some I saw again during business trips and for others this would be the last time.

Adjusting to Remote Status

*"Life is a series of natural and spontaneous changes.
Don't resist them; that only creates sorrow. Let things
flow naturally forward in whatever way they like."*
—**Lao Txu**

My remote career began in September of 2001. On 9/11, we were getting packed by movers. Instead of packing, the movers and our family stood watching the events of 9/11 as the world did. It was a very sad day. We also heard that the cost of gasoline would spike, so that night we stood in a mile-long line at the gas station. Everyone was fearing for the worst. We paid $4.00 a gallon, the normal of today.

We slept on a blanket the last night, just as we did the first time we moved into the house! We had already said our good-byes to our neighbors and friends. Our small family and Puzzles, our dachshund, looked around for the last time, and away we went!

In Tucson, we moved into a small apartment until we found our more permanent home. Our daughter was registered at the same school as her cousin. "You get to go to school with Marisa!" we said, and this is how we convinced her!

We wanted her to continue in a Catholic school, but she hated wearing uniforms and she wouldn't know anyone at the school. It was best to start her with her cousin. This was a good move.

In Colorado, in kindergarten through third grade, Melissa did well in math but in fourth grade, she was assigned a teacher who didn't teach. She sent the kids with homework to have the parents teach them. Half of the class parents wrote to the diocese to voice their concerns. She was also saying things to the kids that were inappropriate.

During a parent/teacher conference, I questioned her teaching method. I explained that we, the parents, should not be teaching the students. Yes, we can help, but not teach the whole lesson. She tells me, "Well, you can serve yourself a glass of wine, while helping her!" That didn't go over too well! There were more things she did that angered the parents; they led to her dismissal. Unfortunately, it wasn't until the summer after classes were over.

Melissa got behind in math and so when she began school in Tucson, I had a discussion with her teacher about her fourth-grade experience so that he would keep an eye on her progress in math. He was great! He helped her regain her confidence. Her math skills improved and later in college, she took summer math classes to further advance.

With our move to be near our families, we were now involved in family gatherings that in some months, were every weekend, and still are. There were birthday parties, graduations, weddings, and then the holidays! In addition, we repeated the same with our in-laws. At one of the first gatherings, Mom asked if we had become alcoholics! Mom never drank and no one else in the family drank that she knew of. We were adults and she was still treating us like children! We just laughed it off and now she'll ask for "poquito" when my husband gets her to accept a tiny bit of beer in a small glass!

From 2001 to the fall of 2004, I continued to gain new knowledge on the Commission systems and was part of the yearly start-up. As in all instances, the Commission's function was the last in training. First Finance, then Production, if the system was going to include shipment schedules with automatic invoicing, then Order Entry to enter the sales, then Accounts Receivables to bill the sales and simultaneously the Customer Master database then lastly commissions to pay the sales reps. Customer numbers were important because our reps were paid differently, depending on who they sold to.

The new global system caused us many issues and became manual. Our division was too small to fit into the big corporate systems. We were just too complex. I worked closely with the headquarters Operation Managers and Analysts. They couldn't understand our company, not even the CEO.

My peers outside of our division, mainly in Atlanta, were called Finance Analysts. They didn't know what to call me, since I handled everything. My duties were that of a Sales Operations Manager, a Commission Analyst, Product Specialist, Sales Plan Implementation, and I also did a lot of Data Mining. So, my title became informally, Sales Operations Specialist.

It was during one of our training travels to Atlanta that Peter finished giving me my appraisal. When we discussed it over the phone, he had to leave in the middle of it. So, on this trip to Atlanta there were a few of us in the elevator and as I remembered, I asked when we could finish my appraisal. We planned that once settled in our rooms we were to meet at the restaurant. During this discussion he told me I intimidate him. He said I knew too much. He gave me the highest appraisal! Intimidating him or not, I was happy!

I was surprised because a few weeks before, I had received a birthday gift from my friend Danica. It was an appointment with a Psychic. Psychic readings are prohibited in the Catholic church, but I didn't think about that until Ana mentioned it when I was sharing the experience. I gave the woman the month, date, year, and hour I was born. That is all I gave her. She then called and spoke to me on the phone for about 30 minutes and told me what she had learned about me. She told me that I intimidated my manager and my dad. She said something happened to me when I was younger and that I was still holding onto it. She told me that I would become a writer. I didn't think anything she told me was a bad thing. Yes, I might be holding onto something, and I knew I liked to write. I wrote many business procedures, so I assumed that was the type of writing she was referring to. Intimidating people, especially people I cared for? I never did this Psychic reading thing again.

The first year I had to perform the yearly start up with additional steps, I was a little nervous, maybe a little insecure, so they brought Dennis in from retirement. I'm not sure if it bothered him that he had to come back or if he was just grumpy because I couldn't do it alone. After a month of his grumpiness, I asked he be removed. I struggled for a little while but with the patience of my corporate counterparts, I was able to understand what I hadn't before.

After struggling through those few months, I decided to create a binder with tabs on every task I had to perform. It was something I could refer to so as not to have to depend on anyone. Soon enough, corporate understood my potential and continued to add more to my plate. I really didn't have a choice since I was the only Specialist in our division's headquarters. I worked closely with the sales team's Business Analysts. I was asked to teach them part of my responsibilities so they could assist me. They were already too busy with their responsibilities, so they weren't given the time to learn the new tasks. I finally gave up and did it myself by working 12-to-15-hour days and weekends. My family could attest to this.

At one point, Peter and another manager and I went to Atlanta to go through a close. We were closing the commission month. This required gathering financial results and sorting through Business Partner reports. Sales Reps were paid on financial data that included sales direct to the customer and Business Partner sales. Business Partners were from external companies that worked hand in hand with our Sales Rep, but the customer purchased the product from the Business Partner. The Business Partner then sent us an Electronic Data Input (EDI) file or a faxed report with thousands of line items that consisted of each sale by account with Address, City, State and Zip Code. My job was to apply the sale for each line item to the right sales rep. I got help for the first two days but then was left alone to finish the week. Peter left early and the other manager and I remained for the rest of the week. When it was time to leave, I grabbed my computer bag and left. At the airport, I discovered that I didn't have my suitcase filled with a week's worth of dirty clothes! It was too late to go back for it. The office manager promised to ship it back to me right away. I felt badly for the inconvenience. She did not allow me to pay for the shipment, so I had my mom knit her a beautiful black silky shawl. She loved it!

So many unusual things happen when one is tired and stressed. Some incidents are just unheard of.

During another trip to Atlanta, I was reading a book on the plane and the woman next to me commented on the title. I don't recall the title, but I know it was one of Nicholas Spark's books. I caught up on my reading when I flew to Atlanta and very sure I purchased the book at one of the airport's shops as I always did. I had just finished reading it when we arrived. I gave it to her, and she was more than happy to take it. This was a one-week trip. On my way back, while in line to board, this same lady walked past me and recognized me. She pulled out the book, handed it over, and thanked me. What are the odds to meet the same person, a stranger, a week later.

One of my favorite Channel sales reps and I were talking one day, recounting all the odd things we have done from being overwhelmed with work. We shared similarities, like looking for keys that are in your hand or sunglasses that you're already wearing. Getting into other people's car was a favorite. Waving at strangers, thinking it was someone you know. My worst was when I was headed to the restroom in a hurry, arms down, slightly swinging them, turning the corner, and hitting an executive right in the crotch. We bumped into each other and that's where my hand landed. Luckily, he was wearing a wool jacket that was between him and my hand. I quickly apologized and went into the restroom. I wanted to die and wished I would never see him again, but he was my third line manager.

System Integration and Loss

> *"It isn't the mountain ahead that wears you out;*
> *it's the grain of sand in your shoe."*
> *—Robert W. Service*

Under Peter, my work was steady until 2004 when the company chose to automate one of our manual processes. It was an exciting moment for me, to be able to learn from start to finish and be part of the new system team. I didn't realize until later that I was project managing my portion of the integration project. It resulted in a lot of overtime since some days were spent on conference calls and so the day work was pushed to the evening and weekends. I was now working solid 15-hour days. Peter also had the responsibility to understand my responsibilities, since they also pertained to other projects he was responsible for. That meant more weekend time with him and resentment from my family.

One Sunday morning when our family attended the 11 a.m. mass, I was still sitting in my pajamas, on the phone with Peter. Melissa came over in her Sunday dress, gave me a look that I'll never forget. She looked so pretty but sad. I heard her and Dad, leaving without me.

The advantage I had in working with Peter is that he read right through me. He knew when I was having difficulties expressing myself when on conference calls. It wasn't so much that I couldn't express myself, it was more that my brain is very detailed, and executives don't want to hear the detail. That was my weakness. I'm not sure I ever grasped the art of summarizing data. Another reason why Peter wanted to learn every aspect of my responsibilities was to determine why I worked so many hours. He and future managers tried to tell me to push back on new requests but in my position that just wasn't a reality.

Since I was the sole producer or employee supporting 100 sales reps, managers, and technical teams, I no longer went on vacation without my computer. I worked holidays and sometimes sitting at the company's site. I remember many years when I'd be pounding the keyboard late at night while all the sales teams were in their comfortable living rooms watching the Super Bowl game.

Shortly after, I received a box with a beautiful bouquet of roses. It was from a manager who was thanking me for my services. I remember this day because it was also one of my birthdays and Mom's friend drove her to bring me a gift. When she saw the bouquet, she commented how beautiful the flowers were. Then I explained who and why they were sent.

"How could the flowers be cut for such purpose?" she said, never congratulating me, nor did she realize that she had hurt me.

This is the year that Mom became a widow. We had celebrated Father's Day at Laurie's home. The whole family was there. This meant about 25+ family members. We were eating and listening to music. At one point Dad stood up and started dancing, so I joined him. The young kids got the biggest kick watching Tata (grandfather) and their tía dance. We sat down and he leaned over and told me he loved me. This is the very first time and last time he would say those words to me. He always said them in letters and birthday cards but never to our faces. Maybe he did to my siblings.

Sadly, three days later, he passed. Mom went to church every morning and the routine was that when she returned, Dad was sitting on the couch waiting for breakfast. This morning, he was not there, and he wasn't in bed. She found him in the bathroom on the floor. She already knew he was gone but didn't tell Laurie when she called her to get help. Laurie had called 911 before she left her house. When she arrived at our mom's home, she found out he had already died. Laurie will carry this scene for the rest of her life.

I didn't cry. I didn't grieve. I don't know if it was because at that time, I was so busy at work and just moved on, or I was holding grudges from when we were younger. I was away from home, already married when he changed for good. I rarely cry, but I do remember sighing for Mom and thinking,

"You are free, mamá!"

Maybe this is the reason for this story. To let go.

A few years later a plaque was mounted on a granite stone in memory of Deacon Roche at St. John the Evangelist School next to the skate park. Dad was involved with the church and the city getting approval to add the skate park to the playground. He had the kids in mind, wanting to keep them out of trouble. He was also a boy scout leader and so he was aware that kids get bored in the summer causing them to get into mischief, so he fought for this skate park.

This same year on December 2nd, Nana Anita passed away. We all went to Rayón for her services. I recall that on the day of her funeral the cousins, including myself, gathered around a bonfire. Right next to us was a calf on a rotisserie and our male cousins were serving us. That was rare, since the women always serve the men. They were breaking tradition. Our mother looked peaceful and occasionally came out and joined us around the bonfire.

In less than a month of my grandmother's funeral, we had returned to Rayón for the New Year's dance. Some of the older women gossiped about us breaking the mourning custom but our mother and those closer to my grandmother had no qualms about our disrespect. This part of the custom became less important to them.

Letter to the CEO

"It's a fact that you're going to have a different opinion
or view on certain topics or issues. You need to stand
your ground by sharing your view."
—Michael Barbarulo

At the beginning of 2005, the new commission system was put into place and introduced to the field. I had my share of training in Atlanta and then had the responsibility to facilitate trainings to the managers and sales teams I supported. Then trouble began when the reality unfolded that the large system was not going to work for our small division. First, we paid the sales reps commissions based on very intricate territories, whereas the larger part of the company paid their reps based on zip code or a whole company regardless of zip code. For example, within our company, we had reps paid on industry codes (medical, manufacturing, construction, transportation, etc.) We paid some by county codes, others by zip codes but not the whole zip code.

Headquarters refused to listen to our complaints that it just wasn't fitting with our territories and sales plan. For the next year, I tripled my hours as I manually corrected the errors that came out of the system. There were days that I literally worked 18 to 19 hours and I recall a few 20-hour days.

In between all this, I had to attend another sales kickoff event, this time in New Orleans. I was to have a Question-and-Answer session with the Sales Reps and the Business Analysts to clarify issues of the new system and what more was to come. We had gone out the night before and I tried to drink one glass of wine but didn't drink much of it because I wasn't feeling right. I was getting dizzy and was constantly cold. I blamed it on fatigue. I was invited to have breakfast with one of the Regions. I was not hungry, so I ordered an egg and toast. I barely touched it. Then I was sent to a large room and I'm sitting at the front. I was shivering, even with a sweater. I wished I had a coat or a blanket. I answered questions as best I could.

When at home, I started feeling numbness on my face and blurry eyes and had no reason for it, even though I knew that I was working too many hours. Finally, one day, my face went numb, and my lips swelled. My husband was traveling so I was alone, and I drove myself to the hospital. When I got there, they first scolded me for driving myself and then they laid me on a bed outside of a hallway since there were no vacant rooms. I must have slept for hours even with the small interruptions for blood work. I remember waking up for seconds at a time and seeing my Tía Amelia sitting at my feet watching over me. I must have called her when I arrived at the hospital. While there, they didn't think to take a blood sample for diabetes. It wasn't until my primary physician took blood samples to determine the cause of my symptoms. I was diagnosed with diabetes. I am sure it was caused from the stress and long hours, but I kept going at it after resting for a weekend.

The system never worked for our small division, but we were continually told that we had to use it. Since I was the one taking the pain and frustrations from the reps and sales executives for the loss of commissions due to the system not working, I decided to write a letter to the CEO. No one else was listening. I had enough of the hours I was combing through thousands of line-items of revenue and machines that had to be manually tied to each of the sales reps' territories then tie those to the technical people and then to the managers. This was a monthly process that was wearing me down.

When a couple of sales managers from the corporate company, whom I did not support, were calling asking me to fix their issues too, I knew I had to do something. My letter to the CEO was simply saying, your big system is not working for our small division; can we go back to using our homegrown system? I also provided examples of some of the hate notes I was getting from the sales teams. I was the dartboard for the executives who were paid commissions. They cried that I was starving their families. If they only knew that their salary was 10 times mine and I wasn't starving. I know the CEO never read my note because I was questioned by one of his assistants, but I am sure it got to the director running the system because within a few days he allowed us to use our homegrown system.

I didn't think of this homegrown system until Thanksgiving when I was putting the turkey in the oven that year. My new manager, Mildred, won't ever forget this. She told me that was an example of what the mind does when it's resting. My mind never rested but she was right. You must give the mind a rest so it can think clearly to improve performance.

One of the executives who was one of the worst complainers turned out to be one of the most loving managers. He is Italian and we used to have arguments. One day he randomly said,

"I would never marry you; you work too many hours!"

"And I wouldn't marry you because you'd complain how I cooked your egg!"

So, we both agreed he was a complainer and that yes, I was a workaholic! I cared too much for the sales team whether they were Representatives or Executives. Some were barely making commissions and for them to not get any because of a system failure just wasn't right!

The East Region was my favorite. I heard rumors that the East Region was the worst and that they were rude. I learned the opposite. The director was a female and was very successful. She worked hard to make her Region be Number One. When her Region came out ahead, she included me in the celebrations. We worked together well. Her Business Analyst, Patsy, was also fun to work with. We spent many hours on the phone. We had disagreements and at one time she said, "Don't yell at me, I'm not your husband!"

We laughed about this for a long time.

She and I were together at one of the sales conferences and were placed in the same room. There was a dinner and dance night at a venue that was reserved for our group. We had the whole place to ourselves but every so often men from the outside snuck in. One man kept asking me to dance. I finally danced one dance with him to get rid of him. He was drunk as a skunk. Right after, I went straight to the hotel room and showered. From then on Patsy teased me that I was dancing all night with dirty old drunk men. She reminded me of that every time we talked.

Poor Communication – Old to New Manager

"Things change. And friends leave.
Life doesn't stop for anybody."
—**Stephen Chbosky**

Now to explain how my new manager was introduced. We had sales kick off meetings in Orlando or sometimes in New Orleans. The year we were in New Orleans, in 2005, I had just arrived from Tucson. I walked into the dining area and one of my co-workers hugged me and announced that I have a new manager. I was so shocked that he had to tell me rather than Peter, my very own manager.

I remember I was angry and hurt. I couldn't look at Peter at breakfast and didn't want to talk to him either, but he grabbed me and took me outside to tell me that he wasn't told either that he would no longer handle the commissions portion of his current position until that week. He then introduced me to Mildred, who was very nice and understanding. I felt bad that she saw how upset I was and didn't want her to think I wasn't willing to give her a chance.

After a few glitches, Mildred and I worked well together. The only thing she pressed me on was to not be so strong in my notes to my customers and headquarters support group. This wasn't new to me. That is what became of me as I became busier and felt it was the only way I got answers about unreasonable deadlines. It was mindless communication! I think I just made that up but it's the best way I can describe the urgency in my notes that maybe did sound strong. I just couldn't afford to waste time! My prior manager told me the same thing, and so did future managers. I told her I was a little rough around the edges but that it was not with bad intentions.

I imagined she grew up in an all-girls' school, wearing a plaid uniform and oxford shoes; but now following her on Face Book, I chuckle to myself as I see her patiently waiting for chicks to hatch and keeping a garden and most importantly, being there for her family! She worked very hard, and I truly admired her. On a personal note, I appreciated so much when she called to check on me when I was sick with COVID. It had been at least 20 years since we talked, other than by Christmas-card exchanges.

I don't know if she finally gave up trying to refine me or just overlooked it. She was the next one who supported me and has always instilled in me that I was better than what I thought of myself. Once again, another manager holding my hand!

During this time, I learned to become a System Business Analyst, not as a title, just the work I engaged in for a couple of months. I was working with a developer from Brazil who was helping me with the Territory Database. We were refining it to make it more in line with our commissions. It required that each manager define each of their Sales Rep's territories. The territories were becoming too intricate. The East Region wanted to break territories down by so many parts. Some reps wanted to be paid on sales to health facilities, others by zip codes, others by county codes, and the list goes on. A simple territory would be by zip code. If a rep sold a printer to numerous customers within a zip code, the rep would receive commissions on those sales. Then we had the Channel Rep territories. Those were assigned by Enterprise. A customer number includes an affiliate number that ties all same customers (i e. Walmart and Sam's Club would share the same affiliate number) then there is the enterprise number. The enterprise number is tied to the Business Partner company. Our division paid internal sales reps, called Channel Reps, commissions for sales made to the Business Partner. So, we had two types of sales reps, those who sold directly to the customer and those who worked with the Business Partner. Not to complicate things, but we had additional layers of Reps and managers, such as technical engineers who assist the Reps in the sales and later at installation of the printer.

Then we had printer categories to consider. There were high-end printers and low-end and later mid-range printers. By the time we were done, we had created what seemed like hundreds of exception codes. What confusion! The many types of territories were going to be a challenge, but I liked the challenge.

It always amazed me how quickly I learned how to design and implement and adapt to new databases or new systems. Sometimes I felt that I could have easily studied Computer Science. I think I would have done well, only if I didn't fall asleep.

I still had to work with Peter on some projects, so we made up and continued to be friends. He helped me get through many of my insecurities in my future assignments. He continued to be there for me when something work-related came up that I couldn't figure out or when I needed guidance. He pretty much kept me from making stupid mistakes at times of manager or bureaucracy conflicts. We continued the friendship but as most work friendships end, ours did too. However, I will always be thankful for his existence in my life.

"Run Forrest Run"
~ from Forrest Gump

"There are only two ways to live your life.
One is as though nothing is a miracle.
The other is as though everything is a miracle.'
—Albert Einstein

I didn't have Mildred as my manager for long because I learned later that she was getting involved in the sale of our division. I was then slowly getting involved in providing the flow of our commission system and the day-to-day processes to the business analyst working with the developers of the new system. I thought it was a good opportunity to request the Project Manager position. I was told I was needed in the position I was currently in and was asked to stay on for at least a year, so I stayed. Since I couldn't be the Project Manager, I was determined to hire someone I could work with. I contacted Josephine, my friend from San Diego and she was hired!

My new manager, Eileen, had not been with the company for long, but learned very quickly, and I loved how she worked with numbers. The highlight with this manager was two things. The first incident was when she added an additional responsibility to pull reports for all geographies, meaning worldwide countries. They needed one report for a meeting overseas. At that time, I was provided reports from corporate headquarters so all I had to do was run the query and then manipulated the results. This was one of two times that I had to pull reports for the world, so I was still learning. I was very sick with a cold, fever, and was very tired from just closing a U.S. commission month. The closes were always a short 12-to-24-hour turnaround.

It was late in the evening, and she had me on the phone pretty much saying, "Run Forrest, run" asking me to stay on with her because the results had to be in by early morning. She had a copy of what I was looking at and was trying to figure it out for me. All I wanted was an Advil and a bed. It felt like my head was going to explode. She finally hung up when it appeared that I was close to finishing the report. I was left with no one to contact. It was late in the evening. I ran into a problem; something didn't balance. The more I looked for the error, the less I could think. What was I going to do? Panicking, I went and stood in front of the crucifix that Mom had brought from Medjugorje, and I screamed in anguish, "I can't do this anymore, help me!" and went back to my desk.

Lo and behold, it was a simple typo! Too many zeros on one of the numbers. You can call it a miracle, or that I just needed to step away. I want to think of it as a miracle because I knew how tired I was and was no longer thinking clearly.

I found out the next morning that there was a delay in the meeting, and it really hurt that I allowed myself to be abused that night.

The second thing: she hired an employee to take over the U.S. commissions to "help" me out. From the start I sensed that he was not the right candidate and really wanted to get Julie rehired. Julie is my friend from Colorado, the one who was at my going away party. I knew her work ethic from earlier years and knew she would be fantastic. My advice was ignored. So, it took 2.5

excruciating years in training this guy and ended up adding more hours to my already overwhelming workload. I did get a nice bonus at the end of the year for my efforts in trying to train him but also for all my efforts in meeting deadlines. Shortly after our first global close he left the company. In the meantime, another manager was hired.

A few years later Eileen said something to me that I will never forget that appeared to be an apology. She didn't come out to apologize for either of the two situations, but I know that she was in her own way saying she was sorry. I felt sorry for her because I knew she was getting a good beating from the executives. She worked very hard and probably still is. I think we could have become closer friends had we not been so busy trying to save the world.

Squeaky Wheel

"Life's too mysterious to take too serious."
—*Mary Engelbreit*

Within two years, our small company had already evolved into a 3-year venture as a subsidiary with another company. We worked on creating our own systems from the bottom-up. This was three years of very hard work. During this time, I was flying back and forth to Boulder. Sometimes, I would stay two weeks at a time. Lucky for me that I had established friends. I stayed at hotels but before leaving for the night, a few of us had dinner or sometimes I'd pick up something to eat at the hotel.

This event needs to be shared because it was so unexpected. I was to meet Danica and Bunker for dinner at their home. Danica was working late. Bunker was retired so he's at home.

"Danica is going to be late, just sit!" he said, so I sat at the breakfast bar, with him in the kitchen on the other side of me. There is a place setting, just one.

"We should wait for Danica." I said, but he refuses.

"May I help you with anything?" Offering to help him in the kitchen.

"Just sit!" he told me, like the Marine he is. It was a command and he continued with the dinner.

Dinner was ready and he served me. I felt so silly to be served! He told me to enjoy it. After a few sips of wine, I was enjoying every bit of it. No one has ever done this for me. He was so proud of himself. Danica was late and so it was a late night but a very memorable one.

Back to the first year after we became part of the new company. To get onto our own temporary systems, I had to build queries for Global commissions. I had no worldwide experience, other than that nightmare night working on the Japan report when I couldn't figure out my error until I demanded help from above. I had to quickly learn how each country did business so that I could customize their queries. There was no time to schedule the experts from Atlanta, so I had to learn as I went. Later I learned that the queries I used in the U.S. could be used for other countries, but the data was to come out of each unique country's financial database. This meant that I had to first obtain access for all these databases and then tweak the queries to customize them for their countries. I had no resources outside of the U.S. to help me with the other countries' queries and system access. The only technical contact I had was from the U.S. The lady was to help me get access to the worldwide systems, but I was not getting the help. She later sent me an email with the information and told me I should stop being a "squeaky wheel." I didn't know what that meant, so in my reply I asked what was wrong so I could fix it. I asked one of my peers what she meant!

I wasn't trying to be funny but after I sent the note and understood how naïve I was I couldn't stop laughing. I truly didn't think I was being unreasonable with my requests. I was just trying to gain access to the queries to move on to the next task to get us ready for the first close.

Commission Close and Sorrow

"Sorrow looks back, worry looks around, faith looks up."
—Ralph Waldo Emerson

I had three months to obtain access for all the analysts plus train them before the first global consolidated commission close happened. I also had to train all the global operation managers on some of the new processes and territory requirements. I was also expected to continue supporting the U.S. sales team. At this same time my niece was dying of leukemia, but I really didn't know how close she was to leaving us. All I know is that I carried her in my heart while I tried to save the first commissions.

This was a very difficult time because I was the only one with this knowledge and I couldn't train the group fast enough. What my peers and probably my managers never considered was that I was teaching myself as fast as I could so that I could quickly train the new Analysts. Never in my years at this company had I dreamed of holding this position, doing work beyond my capabilities. Having Rheumatoid Arthritis and Diabetes made it that much more stressful, but I knew I was "the" person. Fortunately, I was not involved in the actual calculations of the new system. That was one less thing I had to focus on.

Then came the week that the international groups came to Boulder for the training I had to prepare for. I was to teach them the algorithm of the Territory Database and the queries. I was no trainer, and I was stressing. I loved the International Sales Operations Managers. They were patient and understanding. Many couldn't believe what I was put through. Seeing how friendly and caring they were, I fought harder to learn more so that I could help make their learning and operations go smoother and easier.

Around this time one of the new Commission Analysts was mentioning to his peers how impressive it was that I was in this position, despite not having a college degree. It stung.

Our first commission experience was in April of 2008, in a big conference room where all the analysts sat and pulled data and manipulated it on Excel spreadsheets. I was like a teacher going from analyst to analyst as they asked questions. We literally worked 20-to-24-hour shifts. A couple of Analysts worked through the night and only left the building to buy Starbucks to keep them going.

On the last day of close, I still had the Maintenance group that I was responsible for. I took on this group since all the other Analysts were already overloaded with their assigned geographies. They were assigned a group of countries or one or two large ones. When I got to my desk, my phone was ringing. It was my sister Laurie calling me from Tucson. I could tell she had been crying, but she didn't mention that my niece's condition was worsening, so I thought she just needed to talk. I remember feeling worthless not being able to be there for her and was overwhelmed with emotion for both the close and my sister's sadness.

At that moment the manager who was responsible for the group of reps for whom I was closing hovered over me demanding I get their work done quickly. I swallowed my emotions despite being half blind from fatigue. I finished the work on time, but it wasn't perfect. At that point I knew I had done the best with what little energy I had.

The next day someone had to drive me to the airport because my manager knew I was in no condition to drive myself. The analysts figured out what to do with my rental car.

Before I left, I had spoken to Autumn, who also did not let me transfer to a different department because she needed my expertise on her team. She didn't know much about commissions, so she respected my knowledge. I told her I was resigning. I was done with it. I didn't want to come back.

She knew I had gone through a lot in trying to put together the new queries and train the analysts for a semi-successful first run of commissions. I cannot emphasize how difficult this project was. I knew I had gone over and beyond my limit. I had no leadership training, nor any training or facilitating training sessions. She refused to hear about me retiring. She believed in me. She talked me into staying and she worked hard to give me a nice raise and probably my last significant raise. As usual, she knew it was not where I should have been on the pay scale so I had a tiny speck of faith that I could see future raises.

My niece passed away two days after I returned home. The agony I was going through with the first close was nothing compared to the sorrow that my sister and her family were going through. I will never forget when I was told that my manager cried in front of my team when she told them about our loss. This was the first time I felt that my work environment was not surrounded by robots but that there was a human behind it. Thank you, Autumn!

Shortly after, I visited with Fr. Joe. I had questions about grieving and in conversation, I began comparing myself with my siblings and co-workers who had gone to college while I had nothing to brag about. He abruptly stopped me and sternly said, "Do not ever compare yourself with anyone! You were lovingly made by God. If He was pleased with you, you should be pleased with yourself!" That stayed with me throughout the years!

Drama

*"I'm selfish, impatient and a little insecure.
I make mistakes, I am out of control and at times hard
to handle. But if you can't handle me at my worst,
then you sure as hell don't deserve me at my best."*
—Marilyn Monroe

After the first close, our VP of Human Resources temporarily became our manager. During this time a manager accused me of many things. Fortunately, the Analysts defended me. I know he was not happy that the first close was not flawless. What he never understood was the complexity and the fact that I was forced to learn more than I ever asked for in a very short time to be able to train the new Analysts and the global Business Analysts. I literally had no one to train me. I had to spend hours reading, researching, testing, and learning from my errors.

I wasn't the only one he was after. He disliked the three females on the team, me being one of them. At some point, we all started fighting back. It got us in trouble. We were called into the HR office, and we were given a little lecture. We couldn't prove what he was doing behind our backs, so we gave up fighting and let management figure it out on their own which they did in less than a year when he abruptly walked out on us, leaving us with a mess but not before he caused more havoc.

Soon after one of my favorite Analysts also left us with no notice. It was partly that his manager had talked him into leaving. I really liked this guy. He used to call me his "Mama Española." He was smart and worked long hours. I later learned that all the over time was affecting his marriage, and he was a newlywed. It was good he left but I just wish he'd given notice. He moved to be closer to home. He now has a family, and they appear to have a happy life. I am happy for him and his wife and perhaps one day we will meet again.

A few months later our new manager, Paul, was introduced. He knew I was looking for a position outside of our department. He asked if I would stay for a couple of months so I could help him learn the team's function. Here again, I was asked to stay. If you've been keeping track, this is the third time I've asked to be moved to a new position and denied.

Since I worked remotely, I had a disadvantage. There were meetings without me, and I missed many discussions. I was always drilled as to why I recognized errors yet no one else on the team recognized their own errors. My responsibility was to spot-check their work and I knew how to spot errors but couldn't ever explain how, other than the fact I had been doing this type of work for 15 years.

At one time, I was asked how the Commission Analysts were doing with their assigned countries. I mentioned that the U.S. was slow. I never meant that the Analyst was slow. The U.S. country is big and complicated, so it is slow. Then a manager told the U.S. Analyst that I said she was slow. She refused to talk to me after that.

I did okay with my new manager. He didn't really bother me. He admitted that he was okay with me and my work but that he didn't agree with some of my thinking. Whatever! I was starting to get a bad attitude. I didn't want this job anymore, but I couldn't see any way out of it, other than to quit — and I wasn't going to do that.

In 2009, I took 18 days off to go to Europe with my daughter. It was a trip planned a whole year in advance. Paul was going to stop me from going. He said I had not requested approval. Okay, so I know I was naïve, and it never occurred to me that I needed to ask for special approval, other than the usual notification. At that time, it was either in an email or verbally, and the manager wrote it in their calendar.

I was very careful about all the work I was leaving behind. I ensured that I left the consultants with all the information they needed to study the system design. My backup had no issues and so I knew I could leave without a computer for the first time in 11 years. This was also my first real vacation in a long time. For 10 years I was leaving 10 to 14 days of unused vacation because I never had time to take them. I learned after this experience that I would no longer cheat myself of vacation and I never did. The company survived.

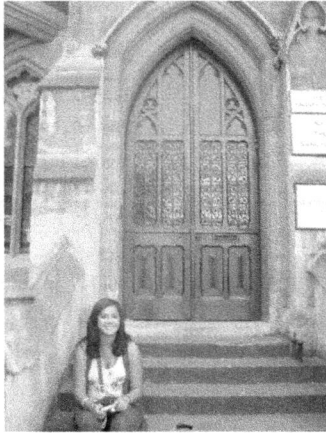

Melissa outside of the Westminster Abbey after mass.

Cafe in Switzerland.

Melissa walking over a bridge in Florence.

Europe Trip

"Food is our common ground – a universal experience."
—James Beard

This trip was at the end of May and early June of 2009. It was Melissa's high school group of 40+ students, teachers, and chaperones. I was just a mother who chose to join the group. We went to London, Paris, and Italy. Our favorites were London and Florence in Italy and Capri.

Florence reminded me of Rayón. It was a Saturday afternoon. The church bells were ringing, and ladies were walking in their mantillas towards the church. We were close by, at the market buying fruit, and I was flirting with the merchant. I didn't think he understood English, so I was telling my daughter and a friend that he was very handsome. Then he hands me our bag and smiling says in plain English, "Thank you, have a good day." And my daughter's reply to me was, "I'm going to tell Dad!"

In London and Paris, we visited many art museums, way too many; the teen-agers were getting bored. In Paris, we were grouped with two boys and three girls. I was also tired and hot and needed something cold to drink. The kids wanted something American to eat. We found a café in an alley to hide from the rest of the group. We ordered drinks and a whole pineapple; then another one. It was the closest thing we could get to American food. We managed to leave without getting caught by the chaperones.

The boat ride to Capri was refreshing. The shops and restaurants were also great. We tried to go to the Mediterranean beaches, but they were dirty. The clean areas were enclosed for the homeowners. We took a tour of beautiful houses and parks and determined only millionaires could live here! Overall, the trip was a good experience, but I would never go with such a big group, especially teen-agers!

Baptismal blessing at the Jordan River with Fr. Joe (left).

The Holy Land Trip

"I've certainly experienced physical pain in my life."
—Katey Sagal

In November of 2009, the same year as the Europe trip, Mom asked if I would go to the Holy Land with her and a church group. I knew it was just a few months since the Europe trip, but I still chose to go. This was Mom's last trip. We went to the Holy Land, Tiberias, crossed the Sea of Galilee, the Dead Sea and the Eastern bank of the Jordan, Jerusalem, and other biblical sites. When we arrived at Tel Aviv, Mom was ahead of me getting off the plane. I stayed behind to grab our bags. I told Mom, "Wait for me at the exit and don't move!" I get down and there is no Mom!

"Have you seen Teresa?" I'm asking all the passengers!

"She's walking with Father Joe," I hear from up front! I run to catch up to her and I am furious. Father Joe looks at me and says, "Relax! She is fine! She's here with me!" I was still furious! If Father Joe wasn't such a nice man, I would have gone on scolding her.

Father Joe Rodrigues is a priest of the religious order of the Society of the Divine Savior, Salvatorians, and currently living and working in Rome. At the time of the trip, he lived in Tucson.

He is also an artist, records new versions of songs and writes some of his lyrics. I own a few of his CDs and occasionally look him up on YouTube for new recordings. His voice is beautiful!

Back to the trip: Mom enjoyed it, while I sat in the bus with an ice bag on my left knee. I had a meniscus tear. I felt it when I took the first step down a flight of stairs on our first field trip. It began after a nephew's wedding. I knew something wasn't right with the knee but brushed if off, thinking it was just sore from the dancing.

I tried to participate in what I could. I enjoyed limping along with Mom in the Dead Sea watching the others swim and play in the water. We had a choice of experiencing baptism in the Jordan River and so I was dunked and baptized by Father Joe. We also drove to the top of Mount of Olives and had a panoramic view of Jerusalem. It was beautiful! Afterwards, I created an album for Mom with the pictures that were emailed and the few that I took. One day, I will repeat this trip to enjoy all there is to see.

The important thing was that Mom enjoyed the trip. She understood enough English to understand the descriptions of the sites and because she knows her bible, she was able to follow along.

I survived the trip by taking four Advil tablets every four hours and keeping ice on my knee when I could. By the time we got on the plane my whole body was swollen. When I finally saw my doctor, she informed me that I had overdosed on the Advil and was lucky it didn't do more harm. A week later I had surgery to have the knee fixed. More time off from work! Not really, though, because I was working from home and worked while healing.

Here I am at one of our Sowing the Seeds gatherings. We are listening to one of the member's stories.

The Writing Group

*"If you're never scared or embarrassed or hurt,
it means you never take any chances."*
—Julia Sorel

Back to personal life in Tucson: After much coercing, I joined the Sowing the Seeds writing group (2009). Ana, my sister, had joined a year or two before. She was impressed with Elena Diaz Bjorkquist, the woman who started the group. She is a published author and so I felt her guidance would be good for me. There were about 25+ members when I began. I had seen Elena at a Book Fair, and she is the one who finally convinced me to join. The group members call each other "comadres." It is used to refer to the mother of the child to whom you are a Godparent. It's also a term of endearment as in being a friend, or better said, camaraderie.

The first meeting was intimidating. I was introduced and all the other ladies introduced themselves as we each took a turn. Each one of them had some kind of prestigious degree. Most were in some educational field. One was a journalist. When it came to me, I stayed quiet because I thought the open introduction was good enough. Elena then asks that I tell everyone a little about my background. I begin talking about corporate work and I can see eyes rolling, not interested. I didn't fit in.

I continued attending and began to feel more comfortable. We were given a prompt and then we wrote for 15 or 20 minutes. We shared the results with the group. Everyone gave their input. Discussions followed but not for too long, especially because we had so many members.

Later we were asked to bring in a written poem, prose, or short essay we were working on. On the day of the meeting, we passed it to the person on the right. We read the piece and added our comments, anything that would improve it. We were taught that good critiquing was helpful for us and to not be offended. If anyone was caught being malicious or hurtful, they were banished from the group. It was a serious group.

Before I joined, they had just published an Anthology book. Everyone contributed one or multiple pieces of their stories, poems, or prose. The year I joined, another Anthology was published and only one piece of mine was included.

I was skipping some of the meetings because of work. Toward the end, the group members kept telling me to retire. I was hearing retirement from many people including from family. Each time I heard it, the more I vowed I would work even longer.

I must admit that I enjoyed the actual writing. I was getting very creative and loved how I could speak better in my writing than vocally. I felt freedom and found that when I was immersed in my writing, I could tune out all my bad energy.

I was looking forward to the next book, but COVID caused our monthly meetings to cease. It was difficult trying to do it via Zoom.

No one ever knew that I was not entirely comfortable in the group. When they gave me compliments on my writing, I kept thinking they were just being nice. One of the members commented that she liked that my stories always included humor and found them unique. The more comments I received, the more I felt they were just feeling sorry for me. I just couldn't get this terrible insecurity out of my system.

When COVID came I was kind of relieved! Then I got the itch to get back to our writing group, but it didn't happen. Most of the members had gone their way. Some started their own groups, and some moved or were just at a different stage of their life that did not include the group!

Back to my work life…For the next two years I worked closely with the consultants and with my peers designing a new customized module (application) that was to be used with Oracle. Having my third opportunity to work with Josephine, I at least had a peer to talk to when things got ugly.

About a year and a half into the design, two of our team members retired. One of them was Josephine, which left me managing the project until another employee was hired to take over as the lead. I had asked why I couldn't be the lead and as usual I was told I was needed where my expertise was. This is the fourth time I was denied a move.

A position opened for a "robust" employee, and Clark was hired. I can't say if he was "robust" or not since I didn't communicate much with him. Thank goodness for Josephine. We kept our friendship, so I kept using her as my sounding board when I couldn't take much more of what was going on at work. By now there were many changes and unfortunately, not for the better.

Big Milestone – 25th Anniversary Celebration

"It is beautiful to express love and
even more beautiful to feel it."
—Dejan Stojanovic

In March of 2010, I celebrated my 25th year anniversary with the corporation, although if you counted all the supplemental years, I would have been celebrating 27 years. When I was looking for a place to have the celebration, I went with Julie, my friend who we hired to be part of the commission analyst group. Her young daughter joined us. We were to inquire about a venue and food at a brewery we liked. A young blonde greeted us. She refused to speak to me. I would do the talking, asking questions. She responded to Julie, who then looked at me wondering why this lady was not speaking to me. I finally figured out that she probably thought I was the nanny. I was Hispanic and didn't look like an office working type of person, you think?

However, I was glad to have found a venue with reasonable appetizer rates. I invited mainly my co-workers and most of my current and a few of my past managers. I also invited another friend who worked in a different department where she had it worse than me. Her 25th anniversary came and went, and management never offered her a celebration of any kind. If I recall, she had a very small lunch with her team months later and only because she requested it. Years ago, the company was much more generous!

My celebration went well! The important co-workers and friends showed up. My team brought in a nice cake! I passed out Brighton key chains to all my female managers and a thumb drive to the male managers. I sincerely thanked them for the past and future years.

After the festivities, we walked to a close-by brewery and had one more drink. My friends thought they were going to get me drunk, but they didn't know I was pouring the drinks in a glass that was right behind me, so I didn't consume what they thought. The celebration went well but there wasn't enough funding, so I ended up paying for most of it, although Paul later insisted on paying me back for some of it out of his own pocket.

A few days later, we had a luncheon, and I was presented with a nice album with letters from many of the people whom I've supported and worked with throughout my years. It was touching and more so because Paul put it together and he is just not the type to do such a thing. I suspect his daughters helped!

New and Last Corporate Manager

"Be careful with what you share with your peers, because one day one could become your manager!"
—Anonymous

During my final three years I went through five managers and finally ended up with one of our team leads as manager. She came into the department 20+ years later, disagreeing with many parts of my tasks, some critical. I was already one or two steps ahead of her, yet she tried to suggest what already had been tried and failed. After some time, I let her do what she wanted only to result in what we had already tried.

For more than a year, Marcus helped me with the design of the new system. Afterward it was discovered that our method was not going to work for another group that had a need to link into our program, so they complained. Karen and Clark thought they had a solution as if we hadn't already tried it. Since they talked like they knew the system and they were superior to me, I let my guard down and let them win their argument and so they undid everything we had created, bragging for succeeding. I just bit my tongue and waited.

A week later it was discovered that their way was not going to work. It backfired. Then they thought they had reinstated the programming to where we had it previously but four to six months later, I was still negotiating the program to be reinstated without penalties. They never admitted it was their doing.

When Karen hired Clark, all new projects were deferred to him. I was no longer a team leader. I was no longer invited to meetings as a team lead. I was never told that I was no longer a team lead, but just slowly pushed aside, left alone out here in the desert.

Sometimes we were given direction on how to perform a task on something she had no experience in, but I would ignore her, and I would do it my way and she never noticed. Of course, I had to be careful since she was the manager, and I was the employee.

As is with many people, this lady was great outside of work. She worked hard but she always left to work just as hard at home with her kids. She may not have known half of my responsibilities, but she was brilliant in what she did know. Perhaps if I had worked in the office, I would have gotten to know a different side of her and would have a different opinion.

Waiting for the Layoff

"When you can't change the direction
of the wind — adjust your sails."
—H. Jackson Brown

Since all the new projects were given to the new employee, I mainly worked with the consultants and with the international Sales Operation Managers and continued to serve as the consultant to the commission analysts. I gave up asking for new challenges because I knew for sure that my time was coming to an end. The owning company started consolidating work at their location to save money on duplicated services. All countries were being migrated to either the corporate office or handled locally. I was left with one country and continued to maintain the system and helped with the commission close.

When the company started working on the new-year sales plan, I was omitted from the planning, whereas normally I was included. There were many projects I was excluded from and so I should have taken a hint much earlier. In any case, I continued to keep myself busy. I wasn't going to let anyone get me down.

About a year before, I had received an anonymous email warning me that he (I'm assuming it was a "he") had heard my manager in a call stating that she wanted to get rid of me. It wasn't true so she tried to find out who the culprit was. To get the techies to trace it, we told them I was frail and stressing out over this. It didn't bother me then but afterwards, I took it to heart. I felt like I was old, too old to be working. This is probably when I started with the bad attitude.

Days and sometimes weeks would go by without a word from Karen. I'm not the type who needs a manager looking over my shoulder, so I didn't need her calling me every day but by golly I wanted to feel part of the team. Thank goodness for Marcus, who I became very fond of. I helped hire him. He called me his second mother. I remember once when he had only been at the company for six months, he threatened to quit. I couldn't see him leaving us because he was one of our strongest analysts. I convinced him to stay. I always had a desire to share my knowledge with someone young who had my passion. Someone who I saw had the potential to make improvements for the department and for himself. Marcus was this employee!

It turned out as I had wished. He remained at this corporation until he was laid off. He worked hard even though he disagreed with some of my processes. I would challenge him to change them, and he tried but only to later see it didn't work. There are some tasks that he did change to make it more efficient. He was very knowledgeable in Math and Excel. These weren't my strongest and so I depended on him to help me with the two. Because of him, I left with more knowledge of Excel that helped me in my next life! We had a good working relationship and because of him I made it through to the end.

While working with him and the developers of the new system, there was one developer we worked closely with. He was not in the office, but we had him on the phone. We were discussing customer numbers and enterprise numbers and how we paid our reps. He wasn't understanding the concept. So, we looked at each other and finally I used an example. I started saying that if he owned Walmart... and then I couldn't finish because I burst out laughing! Marcus looked at me puzzled and couldn't hold back and he started laughing and then the developer began chuckling, but he had no idea why! I think because I could have used a larger company, but I chose Walmart for him. It was silliness but turned out to be a stress reliever!

Julie was another Analyst who I wish would have stayed but by this time, she had made the right move outside of the company. I missed her dearly because she is the one who made me laugh over the silliest things.

One year she was announcing the new sales plan to the global teams. I sat in the meetings to answer questions that were more specific to me. One late evening we were working with Japan. Right before the call, Julie was having technical difficulties and the guy that was supposed to help her wasn't there, so she was cursing out loud not realizing the phone wasn't on mute. We put the phone on mute quickly, but we couldn't stop laughing and when all the Japan participants got on the line, she couldn't compose herself and so came out sounding extremely happy. She pretended to clear her throat when she felt a giggle creeping in, and I finally had to leave the room. She got through the call and fortunately the Japanese team didn't have a clue what was going on.

I received my final appraisal, and my thoughts were confirmed with Karen's last words. It was a very good appraisal! In this last appraisal she praised me for learning the other employees' responsibilities/tasks so quickly!

"HELLO!! I taught that employee what he knows! What do you think I was doing when I was training all six Analysts?" I wanted to shout at her but kept it to myself. I couldn't stand my job anymore but was waiting for the layoff.

One thing that pushed me over the edge was when she got impatient with one of the procedures and steps that were laborious and took hours to accomplish. It was those reports that the Business Partners sent us via EDI (Electronic Data Input) files or emailed Excel sheets of parts sold to specific accounts. The customer names came in different formats. The templates were all unique, so I had to dump the data and sort and manually figure out which sales belonged to which rep. The lists contained thousands of lines. We had previously hired an outside vendor who advertised that they could scrub this kind of data. We worked with them for a few months only to find out that it didn't work.

One month Karen asked that I give the files to Marcus and Clark. She told them with me on the phone to figure out how to do it easier through Excel programs they were familiar with. I just sat quietly laughing to myself because I knew there was no way. I was right so she gave it back to me to continue working with the report. I already had a process I used each month.

Amazingly, a future company I worked for had a much more workable solution and how I wished I knew it then!

Add Mother to the Worries

"Eventually all things fall into place. Until then, laugh at the confusion, live for the moments, and know everything happens for a reason."
—*Albert Schweitzer.*

While I worried about my work as to whether I was going to stay or whether my manager was working on getting rid of me, I had Mother to worry about. For at least eight months, I was taking her to either the emergency room or to her primary doctor or to a specialist. No one could find anything wrong with her, but she was not sleeping nor was she eating, and she was very restless.

Since I worked from home, I became the main designated caregiver. My younger sister had just started working, so she couldn't get out of work. The youngest brother lives far away but has been with the same company for many years and took personal time to help me. My older sister is involved with the public, so it was very difficult for her to help. One brother lives too far, plus slept during the day because he works at night and the oldest brother lives in Minnesota, so he was obviously of no help.

I worked around her appointments, and I started to sense that somebody was keeping track of each time I left work to care for Mom. I couldn't express my personal worries to my mother and so there were many days that I became frustrated and anxious.

There were times when I wanted to throw the phone out the window when I'd get that 8 a.m. call asking I take her to emergency or to make yet another doctor appointment. I was starting to lose it and all I could do was pray for patience and a diagnosis that would lead to proper medication and healing. Thank God for our friend, Cecilia, who has continued to help us when needed. If I absolutely couldn't take her, she would.

Finally, she was diagnosed with serious depression. There wasn't anything that caused it, other than just old age. I felt sorry for her, and it took me a while to let go of the guilt I was feeling for having been so angry and frustrated even though it was done in private.

Mother returned to her normal self. She walks to church every morning. She's cooking for us and back to her knitting and sewing. She's milder and hardly ever nags at us as she used to. We are all happy to see her this way. Even her newly adopted son, who is a priest, told me one day he really thought Mom was in her last days.

Fr. Bardo began his priesthood at the church close to Mom. His parents have both passed on. Mom was the first one he became friends with and began calling her "mom." He enjoys visiting Mom and even takes orders from her. He cooks their meals and cleans up and occasionally will fix something needing fixing. He calls himself her spiritual son. So, in a sense, he's also my adopted brother!

I vowed that the next time I oversee Mom's care; I will be more patient and ask for more help from my siblings. Right?

Not so! I felt so guilty and so for Mother's Day that year I wrote her this letter. I wrote it in Spanish and translated it to English.

Dear Mamá,

This Mother's Day is different. After your suffering last year, I am grateful for your good health. It made me sad to see you downhearted. You, the mother who never tires.

For months we saw you hiding in a cave or bubble. I'd get angry sometimes. Anxiety came from not knowing how to cure you. My smile when with you, hid my sadness. I didn't want to cause you more pain.

This Mother's Day is different. Today we celebrate the days that brought you back, to the mamá we know.

God took care of you when I couldn't take any more. When our work came first, your friends stepped in. Thank you for not faulting me on those days when I couldn't help you.

You think I don't pray, but my prayers kept me sane when it hurt to look at you, the stranger, in depression. My heart died and I moved like a robot as I took you to the emergency room, or to take you to this doctor, or that specialist, knowing you would be turned away with no diagnosis.

Thanks to Dr. Pelayo who spoke to you with tenderness while you sat hunched over without looking at her. She told us depression can come as a part of aging.

What happiness when you started taking the medications prescribed to you. You blossomed into the mother we knew, opening like the petals of a flower blooming one by one, day by day. You finally ate, slept, walked. When yelling and scolding came, we knew you were well, maybe not 100% well, but our mother was back!!

Thank God for doctors, your friends and for the patience He gave us, but we are most grateful for having you back as our mamá, the mother we know and love. Love, Sylvia

The Layoff Call

"Knowing when to walk away, is wisdom.
Being able to, is courage. Walking away with your
head held high, is dignity." —Unknown

I've never been dismissed from a job but when my husband was laid off, I experienced his reaction. He is much calmer than me, so my reaction was 10 times more animated.

At first it was a feeling of anger mixed with humiliation. For me, it was a feeling of failure. I had worked so hard to get myself above my expectations without a degree, thinking I would amount to nothing. To this point, I had felt successful. Then the call comes, and it hits me as if I didn't expect it, yet I knew all along.

The word "frail" came to mind, so rather than getting angry all over, I vowed that I would continue my career and would become more successful and satisfied than the last two years.

It was in June of 2011 when half of my peers were laid off due to downsizing and that is when I realized I would be next. I could have retired but I would have forfeited my severance pay, so I waited out the layoff announcement and sure enough in late February 2012, I received a call from my manager. It was the worst call, even though I "thought" I was ready for it.

She mentioned she had an HR representative on the other line. I thought it was the most unprofessional, cruelest way to announce that I was chosen for the layoff. She then proceeded to explain that the company would be more profitable, blah, blah, blah. At that moment I didn't care to know about the company being profitable and I knew she was reading a script. She asked if I understood what she had said and all I could say is "yes" forcefully and very coldly. Then she asked if I had any questions and I said "no" and that was the end of the conversation. What hurt the most is that 30+ years of long days, late nights, struggles, challenges, and years I could have enjoyed with my family, ended in a 5-minute phone call. Well, those were my immediate thoughts!

The other thought was that I thought I had done something wrong, but the only thought that came to mind was that I had recently asked for a raise when I was asked to handle all the work that Julie left behind when she left the company. I didn't want to push back. I was just finally doing what so many managers had advised me to do. They all thought I worked too hard and told me to push back and quit accepting more work. So, I tried it and it backfired on me. That was my first thought but when she told me on the phone that the projects, I was handling were no longer in existence and that I was now only handling one country that would soon be gone. I wanted to ask if she knew what else I was working on, but I didn't care anymore.

Later when we received the separation package, we noticed the last page listed the ages of those who were laid off, just a tally by age group. To HR it was to prove that it was not an age discrimination deal, although 75% were 50 and older. I still wish I knew the whole truth but that would be playing with my insecurities, and I would rather think of all the managers that encouraged me throughout my career. All I know is that my departure was not as the one when I left Colorado to work from home.

I was left in a daze, not knowing what else to do, so I sat and cleared all my personal notes from the company computer. It took me five hours before I knew I had not had water nor eaten lunch and it was already dinner time. I also prayed and thanked God for freeing me from this place and from people who would hold me back. I asked for help in finding something low key, something I would enjoy doing. I had faith and I knew it would come.

Once notified of the layoff you are treated as if you do not exist, but they want you to perform as if nothing has happened with a threat that if you do not perform, the severance pay offer will be withdrawn. The remaining employees whispered amongst themselves, wondering who that one employee in their unit had been laid off. When I heard this, I immediately sent a note to all employees and copied my manager and the second line manager. I simply told my team that I was the one laid off. I told them I was at peace, and I asked them not to treat me as if I had a disease as I know that's how employees treat those who are victims of these unfortunate circumstances.

For the next month, I created process documents for the two remaining employees left handling whatever was left of my tasks. I prepared an external hard drive to ensure they had all the important data. I can kick myself now because I really could have kept some documents that would have helped me in the future. I sent all the documents in a large note and copied my manager and the VP of HR because I didn't want anyone saying that I didn't leave clear instructions. I left them with my life.

My immediate and extended family celebrated with me. They hated the hours I worked. Why did I do that to myself? The only answers I have is that I became intensely focused on the challenges I faced and once unraveled, passion took me to the next. I was loyal to the company, managers, my peers and to myself. Proving that I could do it without that degree!

I wasn't done yet! My Creator saved me the best for last.

Switzerland and Luxembourg

"If you reject the food, ignore the customs,
fear the religion and avoid the people,
you might better stay at home."
—James Michener

The last trip we took to Europe was to pick up Melissa. She was studying abroad at Les Roches School of Hotel Management. She enjoyed visiting close-by areas including the Netherlands. We met up with her in Crans-Montana, Switzerland. We flew into Zurich and took a train to a small town where we stayed the first night. We were exhausted and hungry. We found a small family-owned Italian restaurant. They didn't speak English and we didn't speak Italian, so we had to guess at the menu items and used sign language. Our meals were delicious. I have never, ever had such good Italian pasta anywhere. I've tried looking for something similar but still can't find it! We went back to the hotel and took a snooze that turned out to be a four-hour nap. After our nap we decided to look for a place to have a glass of wine or beer. The only place we found was a small tavern. The bartenders were drinking and in good spirits. They didn't understand us, but we figured all they had was wine, so wine we had. They smiled at us and pointed to a table, one of three where we sat.

The next day we took the funicular to get to the campus where Melissa was waiting for us. The funicular is a railway that goes up the sides of a mountain; it was originally made to go up steep hills and to carry skiers.

The highlight of the trip was in Zermatt and Luxembourg.

Zermatt is a mountain in the Pennine Alps. The tourist attraction is the gondolas that takes one to see the Matterhorn up close. Ralph and Melissa went up and I stayed down. I do not like heights and so I stayed in the town to do some shopping. After a while, I sat to people-watch when suddenly, a funeral procession came by. I decided to join it so I could get a view of the church which I assumed was the destination of the procession. This was another memory of Rayón. I also saw many St. Bernard dogs. They were everywhere. The food and pastries were also great!

We went to Luxembourg to find Ralph's uncle's grave. Ignacio Dominguez was involved in battles in WWII and was buried in the Luxembourg American Cemetery. To get to the cemetery we took the train from Switzerland. As we are passing by some of the small towns, we see a billboard with an advertisement of the Morales Sisters coming to town. What a coincidence to find this advertisement. The Morales sisters are my brother-in-law, Phil's, cousins. They go on tour with their music.

To get to the cemetery, we get off in Luxembourg and take a bus. Since Melissa had been in buses during her school adventures, she knew what to do. We get on the bus and stand in the back next to the door. We are dropped off about a mile away from the cemetery. There is no other transportation to get us closer, so we walk. As we are walking it occurred to me that we didn't pay for the bus trip. Melissa announces that it's because we came out the back door and there was no one to take our money. Now I'm wondering if they snuck out of all their bus rides.

We walk to the cemetery and view Ygnacio's grave, paid homage, took pictures, and then walked over to General George S. Patton's grave. We were so fortunate to have had this experience and much more for Ralph. We rushed out of the cemetery to catch the last bus run. This time, we paid the bus driver.

And this was the end of our big trips and back to work.

Post Layoff

"Never be afraid to trust an unknown future to a known God." —Corey ten Boom

Soon after the layoff I loved not having early phone calls and not having to worry about the anticipated layoff call. Instead, I went to the gym and listened to a James Patterson audio book while on the elliptical machine. While I listened intently, there was a sudden gunshot (in the story), and it made me jump and startled the guy next to me. I cracked up laughing and quickly explained. That was the last time I listened to a book. It felt good to laugh again!

I didn't start looking for work until three months after my layoff. Boy is it a challenge! My past is made up of corporate education. Some skills fit and some don't. Once I started to apply out of the state for positions identical to mine, I got hits, but I couldn't find a company that offered the benefit of working remotely. I was persistent and had faith that something would come soon. If I didn't have a daughter right out of college, with an education loan balance, I wouldn't sweat it, but education is expensive. I needed to work to not tap into our retirement fund.

Casino Night

"Success consists of going from failure to failure
without loss of enthusiasm."
—Winston Churchill

One of the first big projects I immersed myself into was a
Casino Night fundraiser for my niece, Marisa Ann Gallego,
"*i* MAG *ine* a Cure for Childhood Leukemia" foundation. It was
on April 18, 2012. She would have been 21 in August of this same
year. The event was on the anniversary day in which she passed.

The Casino Night fundraiser was a success. Organizing the
Christmas party in San Diego many years before was a precur-
sor to this fundraiser. Not working, I had the time to lead the
event, as the Director of the Board. I was collaborating with the
foundation board members, taking votes on every aspect of the
venue, food, and activities. Each member was responsible for a
part of the event. Once the venue, caterers, casino, decorations,
etc. were in place, I also put together the silent auction.

All members participated in sending letters to organizations
requesting sponsorship and/or donations for the Silent Auction.
Marisa's family and my husband helped with the final detail of
the center pieces, pouring water into the glass vases, and lighting

the floating candles. We still laugh about this. We had one small pitcher, so my husband had to run back and forth from bathroom sink to the tables. He asked we never again ask him for help as the water boy. I know he'll do it again in a heartbeat.

There were 115 sit-down guests plus all who participated in the silent auction and the casino games. It was a success. We presented the University of Arizona Foundation with $10,000 to support Pediatric Hematology and Oncology Research at the Steele Children's Research Center. The rest was saved to award an aspiring athlete and student help with his or her future education. These students were from the high school that Marisa went to. I hope that with my free time, I can help organize another big event, perhaps to celebrate her 40th heavenly birthday.

Creativity and Theater

"There are far, far better things ahead than any we leave behind." —C. S. Lewis

Being away from work encouraged me to write and read and work with clay without guilt. My creative side was slowly being released. Elena, our writing group's director, was not only an author but was also very creative in other ways. She was an artist and loved sharing her talents. She was teaching clay classes, so I joined her sessions. It was another therapeutic event. This group was much smaller. The most I saw was about six women. We listened to music as we shaped our lumps of clay into whatever our minds guided our hands to create. It was fun while it lasted. I became busy again!

Before looking for new employment, I even thought of selling my salsa and baklava that many have enjoyed and have asked why I wasn't selling it. I found that it was too troublesome, with too many rules, and so I decided against it.

For entertainment my husband and I began buying season tickets for the Theatre, joining Ana and her husband, Phil. On the first night I had an experience that went like this:

263

My sister walks up to pick up her tickets at the "will call" window while my husband and I walk to a waiting area to get out of the way. Two women caught my attention, as they are eyeing us. They are sitting at a dry fountain's wall, staring at us up and down, clueless that I'm watching them. They then turn and stare at my sister and her husband the same way. I recognize that stare. I have mixed thoughts, but unfortunately, the negative thought won as I smiled at them, and they turned away as if they were insulted. Thank God that I made my husband take off his faded jeans and replace them with khakis and shoes in place of his tennis shoes. I thought I looked nice, but it wouldn't have mattered what I wore this evening.

I continue to glance over and wonder how much longer they were going to stare. At one point, I stared right back as if playing a game with them. I was thinking that their clothes probably smelled like mothballs. Then at that moment my brother-in-law, who is legally blind, is walking toward us with magnifying glass in hand looking for the seat numbers on the tickets. The women looked even harder with curiosity, wondering who we were and why we were there.

We turned away to enter the building and I followed behind, not sharing my anger. Fortunately, the woman passing out the programs greeted us with kindness and ensured we took a program. This attentive and pleasant lady immediately changed my mood.

Then we get to our row and find that we must walk over a few people, and I see that I will be seated next to a gentleman. For the duration of the play, I find myself covering my mouth to cover up the lingering onion smell from a wonderful dinner we had just moments before.

The play, "The Importance of Being Earnest" turned out to be entertaining and momentarily hid the unpleasantness brought on earlier by two women who knew nothing about us, yet they thought they knew everything!

It's only those few people who make life unpleasant. It's hard to ignore them sometimes, like going to the grocery store on my side of town. The shoppers glare at you until you move out of their way. They also go in and out of the wrong lanes when leaving the store. Once, I encountered an elderly man turning against traffic on the main road, driving toward me. I moved aside as if it were a normal thing.

Interviewing

"Often what may appear as a detour in life is actually the most direct and empowering path to your destination." —*James Arthur Ray*

With the layoff, we were eligible to file for unemployment after our severance pay ended. It was very challenging looking for work that fit my expertise. After many attempts, I decided to go to a Job Fair. I found a couple positions I applied for. One of them was at one of our school districts. I thought that might be an easy Admin position, so I applied for it. The morning of the appointment, I had no desire to go for the interview. I knew it was not the place I was looking for, but I went anyway.

During the interview, I sat in a room with the director and two technical guys. At one point, I was walked over to an empty desk. There was a huge screen and an old desktop computer. The software was so old that I couldn't understand why they were so behind. They asked me to write a memo to the staff introducing myself. I thought that was strange, but I typed it. My gut told me I was in the wrong place. We went back to the interview room. They seemed interested and I was hoping they couldn't read my face. I later received a nice letter that they had offered the job to an internal candidate. That made more sense to me. I was glad it wasn't me.

From the fair I also met with a local newspaper recruiter. They took my information and continued looking elsewhere while I waited for a call from other companies where I had applied.

I was called in for an interview at some educational facility on Oracle Road. I had never seen it, even though many times I have driven past it. It was an old building but inside it was newly painted and very clean. It reminded me of a hospital that was then converted to an administrative building. Going into the hallway there were two big swinging doors that opened like hospital doors.

I was walked to an office, with two young men waiting for me. They must have been in their late '30s. They drilled me on my Excel and Word skills and had me create a document. They were surprisingly satisfied. We continued to talk when suddenly, I felt faint. One ran to get me water, but I knew I needed something with sugar. Once I felt balanced, I asked for gum or candy. Most offices have someone that brings junk food in, so I wasn't embarrassed to ask. Sure enough, they came with some hard candy. They asked if I wanted to reschedule the appointment and I refused. I was not interested in this position and was never contacted. I was fine with that.

Because I had endured so much stress in my previous dealings, my health was beginning to deteriorate. The worst thing I could have done was to not eat anything before the interview. I had gone without breakfast and lunch and so my blood sugar dropped.

The newspaper called and so I went for the interview. I had a terrible cold and could barely breathe. I was feeling okay, but the cold and cough lasted longer than usual. When I was walked into the CFO's office, I was surprised to find one of the members from our church. I didn't know his name, but we always greeted each other. We chatted briefly, then started the interview with him and the Operations Manager. They wanted their programmer available, but he was out sick.

I thought the interview went well except they required some accounting experience. I knew some accounting and some financial methods since commissions were paid based on financials in most cases. I told them I could teach myself accounting. I didn't mean I could get a degree by teaching myself. I just knew, from the past, that I could learn almost anything related to my tasks. They were looking at my resume, so they were interested in other aspects of my past experiences. They seemed interested but when they asked if I knew the streets of Tucson, I told them not at all. I knew myself well enough that learning the Tucson streets was nothing compared to all the global and U.S. streets I knew from shipments and maintaining customer numbers. I didn't say anything but afterward I kicked myself for keeping quiet. The Operations manager took me on a 30-minute tour of the plant. I kept thinking that if they weren't interested, he wouldn't be wasting his time.

Two days later the programmer called to finish the interview. He asked what systems I used. I told him I used MMS for many years. He asked what software we used, and I froze. I couldn't think what it was. In fact, it's the system and software that we used for calculating commissions in the early '90s. We had lists of queries used for setting the compensation plan at the beginning of the year and another set for pulling sales reports. I stumbled and so I appeared to not know enough. This is when I once again wished I had been formally educated.

I couldn't find anything else that matched my skills, so I applied with a temporary agency. I was called soon after because they had just received a job post for a position involving Rebates and Admin Fees. The recruiter shared with me that they had no understanding of what my previous tasks were, nor did they know what the company posts meant but they figured since their system picked up my resume based on Rebates, I qualified for the interview. They set up the interview date and time.

This didn't surprise me. This is exactly why Target, Walmart, Macy's, and other small companies I tried applying at told me

I was overqualified. I think it was more so because they didn't understand my skills.

My goal was to find an easy-going job with no stress. I was open to a part-time position. I had processed rebates in San Diego, and I continued to process more in Boulder. I felt confident. The CFO, Donald, interviewed me first. He was a very kind man who slowly explained the requirements and the detail of the position. Everything he described was right down my alley. He then announces that I would be interviewed by the CEO, Jack.

He walks me over and I wait for the CEO for a few minutes in his office. I am taking note. His office is in disarray. Manuals and papers were spread over his desk. Opened boxes on the floor. Paper hanging out of his tall metal cabinets. I'm wondering who this man is. Finally, he walks in. He is dressed just like his office. His shirt tail almost hanging out. He's wearing khaki pants that are now wrinkled after wearing them all morning. He is very friendly, shakes my hand and we sit. The interview begins. He tells me the importance of the Rebates and Admin fees. I didn't ask questions about the company because the CFO had already answered the questions. I ask him other questions about the work. The interview doesn't last long, and he dismisses me after talking personal stuff, family, pets, etc.

I went home to begin packing to go to Melissa's graduation from NAU (Northern Arizona University) in Flagstaff. We arrive at a rest area, and I get the phone call. The Temp Agency tells me that Jack hired the other applicant because he had asked about the company and I'm sure for other reasons. They mentioned that if the new hire didn't work out, they would call me back. I was well qualified. I was so disappointed and was on the verge of crying, but I sucked it up and hoped there would be a change in mind.

About a month later, I was called back by the temp agency. They asked if I would consider working part-time at the medical company. I gladly accepted it but had to interview with the CFO once again. It was just for formalities to ensure I understood the tasks and responsibilities.

I learned that the rebates and Admin fees had fallen behind. I was to team up with their new hire to help bring them up to date. He also wanted to be sure that I was not holding a grudge with the new employee for being hired over me. All worked out well. I learned the process and routine.

During this time, the new employee turned in his resignation. They offered me the job full-time through the agency. There was not much to learn from him since I had already gone through the cycle for two months. I felt comfortable. The admin fees were monthly with a few quarterly and it was the quarterly that I would need help with. Donald assured me that he would assist me.

Before this full-time position was offered, I received a call for a similar job at a waste disposal service company. It was a position I applied for immediately after I was denied the first time at the medical company. The position was a Commission Analyst position, supporting a few sales reps and the director. The interview included the senior sales reps and the sales director. It also included the departing Commission Analyst, whose position I would take. The interview went very well.

"I have one last important question," said the director. "If you were at dinner and asked for a medium well-done steak and the server brings you a medium rare steak, what would you do?

I didn't think for a second, "I wouldn't care, I would eat it."

"Good answer!" she said, and the whole room chuckled.

I was offered the job. I needed to think about it. I was excited because this position was very familiar to me. I had shared with them that I was working part-time.

I had to make my own decision. I knew that I initially wanted an easy-going job, and I was in that position. I called the director back and asked if she could up my beginning salary, thinking if I got a better offer, I would accept the position. She couldn't go higher, so I declined the offer. I didn't know if I had made a mistake but at the end, everything went as it was meant to be.

Just before or even during the first month at this new company, Tía Chalita passed away. There were many men and women at the funeral. I observed that the men participated more in what only the women did years ago. It was also more of a celebration. It could be that this lady had such a happy spirit and was very close to the church teachings and wanted nothing less than a celebration of her new life! It was still sad to say good-bye to our chef. This was the last time I went to Rayón.

The Beginning of the End

It's less about learning new things and more about letting go of the old things. —Liza Miller

My new job and responsibilities were perfect. I learned what I needed to do and soon began receiving emails from our customers expressing how satisfied they were with my work and especially the timeliness. I made sure to pass them on to Donald, who I assumed is the one who passed them on to Jack.

One day, Donald called me into his office to ask if I would consider taking on the Commissions function that was currently held in Chicago. It was Jack's idea. I thought about it for one second and explained that I didn't wish to get into a stressful situation. I was convinced that I would only support 30+ sales reps plus the sales managers and the work would be light. I eventually accepted to take on the additional work. After all, when the rebates and admin fees were all caught up and I was in a good routine, I found myself idle during the last half of the month waiting for data from the Business Partners.

The training began. At times, I thought it had been a mistake. The person training me was out multiple times and so it was hard to learn the process in pieces. Eventually, I learned enough to have everything turned over to me. I made changes to what made more sense to me, using techniques from prior experiences.

I also worked with Mack; he worked with Jack and later became the VP of Sales. I took direction from him, also. He is the one I turned to when I was afraid to ask Jack something or needed his help with irresponsible reps. He always put me at ease. Daphne, the International Sales Rep, also worked out of Chicago and was one of the very first employees who was employed with the company. She wore many hats. She also gave me direction and we later worked helping each other.

No need to explain my tasks, it began with the same routine, having accurate customer numbers, keeping up with commissions and dispersing them on time. The biggest difference was that now I needed to learn Access. I had used Access to input data years ago, but never to the extent that this company used it for. The Chicago IT was an older man who soon retired. He was the one who taught me, beginning with the rebates and then with Admin Fees. It was simple once I understood the tables. I had already learned some since that is where the rebates reside. I had initially sat in the same cubicle with the HR Administrator. She was handling part of the Rebates process and so she taught me how to look up Rebates in Access.

Eventually, our data got so big, plus the sales managers and sales reps needed better systems to view their sales and track customer information. An internal employee began the programming in Access, but it was not going to include all features. We ended up looking for a developer. My nephew was hired to do the job. I provided the algorithm and guided him through the steps. The sales managers were also involved. On a side note, when things got hard or I didn't understand a step of the program and had to keep asking for direction, I begged him to not treat me like a client instead of like his dear aunt, but to my dismay, I was his client.

In these late years of my working career, I quickly mastered Access, new financial systems and the enterprise networking systems including the one I helped design for commissions. Wish I could send this to the newspaper's programmer. Ha!

During my time at this company, I learned that it ran quite the opposite of the big corporation. Many would have been fired instantly for speaking rudely or for disrespecting their employees. There was also a lot of cursing, and everyone just kept on with their tasks as if it were normal. It was quite amusing, but all these employees were still producing good results.

Here are a few experiences. Sitting with Leslie, the HR Admin, was unusual considering her handling personal information. I must have looked trustworthy to be put in the same cubicle. Leslie and I worked well.

I'm going off track here but feel the need to include these thoughts. These are like those I had as a younger child. That one day, I would have enough for myself, and I would share with those who didn't just as Anne and Rose's parents shared their wealth with us many years ago with the hand-me-downs. Then we had the food bags that we received from some organization and all that other people did for us when we had little.

During the holidays, I heard of an employee who was having financial problems. I always get sentimental and emotional when I hear things like this especially during the holidays. I immediately asked Leslie if the company could write a check for the amount that I wanted to surprise the employee with out of my own pocket. I didn't want her to know it was from me. Finance did not allow it but better yet, Leslie offered to contribute and so it was more money between the two of us. It was given anonymously. It always feels so good to reciprocate and it doesn't have to be big, nor does it need to be monetary.

Once I was moved to the cubicle that was vacated by the prior employee, I sat right next to the Accounts Receivable and Purchasing groups. There were some discussions going on when suddenly, I hear one of them shout, "Chingado! (In English, it was the F word!) My back straightens, and I am beyond shocked.

This was common. I also met a lady who was shaking. It looked like she had been running. She was very friendly, and right away explained that she has a constant body-tremor problem that has not been diagnosed. She joked about it and later as we became closer and knew each other better, she made terrible jokes about her shakes. We enjoyed each other's company and always had a reason to laugh about.

I was so grateful when she helped me once in the restroom. I was wearing a long skirt. I was washing my hands when she comes out of a stall and comes right behind me and pulls my skirt out of my underwear, as we both laughed. It brought me back to my bus experience when my dress crawled up my behind.

I worked closely with her and the other Accounts Receivable administrators on invoice issues. Later, she was assigned a manager, whom I also later worked with on big Rebate and Admin Fee issues. This manager and I also became friends.

Later, I became close with the Purchasing ladies. They were my go-to for supplies and for companionship. I needed someone who was not associated with my day-to-day activities. One of them makes the best soups. Occasionally, she would bring me a container with warm soup. It is good to have friends who keep us sane (and nourished).

As in the past, I was to learn new personalities and work to understand them to better engage without fear or intimidation. This time it was with Jack. He never showed anger when I made an error if I admitted it. I worried more than I needed to. He would say, "Fix it and we'll adjust next month." Or it was just fixed right then. The more I worked with him, the more confident I became.

He reminded me a lot of my Dad. He was moody and sometimes very angry, but I knew he had a soft side and was not what some portrayed him to be.

Like my brother-in-law, Delbert, Jack knows I'm gullible and plays with it. He talks and talks, and I listen believing everything he tells me and after a few minutes he sees that I'm truly believing every word and then tells me he's kidding. Sometimes he'll keep at it while on the phone and when I hear Mack laughing in the background, I know he's pulling my leg. It's good for a minute of laughter.

We bumped heads on a few occasions, and other times we just compromised! I had the utmost respect for him and would do anything for him, to a point.

Jack had wanted me to take on a pricing project. It was going to be ongoing. It was to filter the special prices offered to the customers by the sales reps. I had never worked with special pricing, but it looked easy enough. Daphne was handling it and so she had a template with the calculations already coded, so all I needed to do was plug the numbers in. I still needed to understand it to feel comfortable, especially when it came to the margins. A few times I had to interrupt him to get his help. One day, I needed his opinion and approval on one of the special prices. I didn't like bothering him, but I needed to learn this new task. He was busy but he took the time to explain. Thereafter, it was a breeze.

There was only one time when I was so sure of myself and was challenged. I had become proficient in all aspects of my job, I was confident enough to know at what point to allow commissions payments to a sales rep's commission statement. Plus, it wasn't any different than at the prior company. One rep went to Jack complaining he didn't get paid for a sale. Jack calls from the Customer Center, "Why wasn't this deal in Jared's commissions?"

I look it up and respond, "Well, it shipped and invoiced but one day too late. He'll see it in next month's commissions." Not satisfied, Jack has me take a printout of the invoice. When I get to the center, he had his buddy, the Customer Center Manager, look up the purchase order. All the Customer Service Reps are listening. They are in the middle of entering orders, so it is quiet except for Jack and the Customer Center Manager who repeats that it had not invoiced in the Commission month. I grab the paper out of his hand.

"I guess I don't know what I'm doing!" I said as I stormed off. I was so angry that the rep didn't come to me first and secondly because Jack didn't trust I knew what I was doing.

At my cubicle, I went to look for my purse to leave. The Rep stopped me and apologized. Then I purposely ignored Jack for the rest of the week. When he was leaving, he came by to beg me not to be angry with him for the next two weeks while back in Chicago. I stood up and don't know what possessed me to reach over and hug him. We made up!

The employees around me couldn't understand how I could work with him and some of the sales reps. They didn't understand my drive. My past 40 years left more bruises than any I would get from working for him and others. I still saw my father in him. Not that I saw him as a father figure. Not at all. It was the personality. We did work out a few more disagreements.

Another "opportunity" was to go through orders with errors. Customer Service had a bin that was used to keep orders that had pricing or product errors. No one was working them, so Jack asked me to monitor the bin. I learned with his help. The Customer Service Reps (CSR) understood what the error was, but they had no control over what was missing or incorrect in the system.

To help me through the errors, I worked with a lady who worked from her home in North Dakota. She handled new parts and ensured they got into the system. She worked with one of our IT guys. If it was a pricing error, it was on me. Sometimes it was just a system problem and something the technical guys had to figure out.

So many times, while working at this new company, I wondered how my life would have been if I had worked there 30 years before. Maybe I would have been fired or I would have learned much more but it was all good timing.

My manager left me to do my work and only sat by me after I calculated the commissions. He was good with numbers and so it was easy for him to find anything I missed. He and Jack had a calculator planted in their brain. They amazed me!

As I write this, so many things come to mind. How did I learn so much, starting at such a young age, not knowing the business world. Then knowing it just enough to get me through 40 plus years. My vocabulary became business words, all related to my tasks. It is hard to get into normal conversation. I used to tell my husband that when I retired, I was going to buy the Rosetta Stone English version! In fact, it will help me learn to pronounce many words. For example, I avoid the word "worm" because it always comes out as "warm" no matter how hard I try. One day as I was speaking with Mack, he was telling me that after a call we had with Jack, I had referenced something on a sheet we were all looking at. I had mispronounced the word, but they understood what I was saying. He laughs, saying, "It sounded so cute!" and I'm getting embarrassed, but he was loving it.

Sometimes when people criticize others who have speech impairments or a limited vocabulary, even if not talking about me, I immediately put myself in that category. For example, one day Jack and a senior sales rep that I worked with were discussing hiring an administrator to take over part of this rep's projects. One of the criteria was that they had to speak good English. I took offense to that even though it was not about me. I tried to brush it off, but it stayed with me for a very long time.

I know Jack also thought I was shy and quiet. It might be my imagination but when he and I were in a meeting with others, I listened to the discussions but sometimes I had an idea or needed to mention something, I'd slowly speak up and then Jack would suddenly silence the room to listen to me. That always made me nervous.

Sometimes, though, I was in la-la land. One time, it was just Jack, my manager, and me. We were discussing my workload and then Jack went off into another topic. I was staring at him, but I was in another world. Suddenly, he asked me a question and I was still not listening. I apologized for not hearing the question.

"Where was your mind?" he asked. He probably never had this happen to him before. Everyone listens when the CEO speaks!

What amazes me is my retention — or lack of it. When I read a novel or the news, I can only remember parts and so I can't ever give detail, yet I am very detail-oriented at work. I can multi-task and remember almost every aspect of the 10+ tasks I was responsible for at all companies I worked at, past and current.

Another problem I encountered is that very few people understood the detail of my job. They cannot comprehend how I keep everything in memory to be able to multi-task. It came as second nature to me, maybe because it was repetitive while I was executing the tasks, but each resulted in a unique way depending on a rep's territory and assigned accounts.

During my entire career, when asked what line of work I was in, I always hesitated. I knew I would bore them with the detail. Mom was clueless but Dad had some understanding from what he experienced in his career as an inspector at the base. My mother-in-law always made me feel that my career was nothing compared to her nieces, the banker and the teacher, and her daughter, the nurse. I had to shrug it off because she too didn't understand the magnitude of the detail, nor how important my service was to the sales group. I didn't blame her. Al, my brother-in-law, understood me more because he was in sales for part of his career. Even my husband was learning my lingo and teased me that my vocabulary was Rebates, Commissions, and Admin Fees.

Becoming a Supervisor

"Plant your garden and decorate your own soul,
instead of waiting for someone to bring you flowers."
—*Jose Luis Borges*

I inherited more work from Chicago. One project was to scrub data. We exported thousands of customer records from Access. We needed to add or delete data from the customers' accounts. We called this "scrubbing data." We were trying to create a database to track sales and at the same time have an accurate reference to the account. For example, a hospital may be listed as part of the Banner Health System for years but now the hospital is under Tucson Medical Healthcare. It was very detailed work, going through thousands of records, Googling the hospital name to get to the most current health system name. Eventually I had to request help. If I didn't speak up, no one would have noticed that I needed help. Help was approved and so I began to build a team. I hired Bernadette first to help with the scrubbing. She too, got overwhelmed and bored with the process. I then taught her to do Rebates so that she wouldn't get bored and leave us. We hired a temporary person to help with the data and finally hired another person through the temp agency. This employee was very eager. She loved to sit by me to learn what she didn't need to learn, but she was so curious that I let her. She later left to go back to school.

For a few months, it was only Bernadette and me, sitting in a small open area. We were away from everyone. We had our own microwave, printer, and a small refrigerator. We brought food from home to share. This worked out for a short time, but the work was growing, and I finally found someone to help with the data. Bernadette was very entertaining. We had many laughs even after we were moved to separate cubicles.

Our Data Analyst turned out to be perfect. Clarissa was a single parent and knew that she really needed this job. She was very happy to work with us, especially with me! (I just made that up!) Seriously, she was happy and worked hard. She loved scrubbing the data because it was quiet work. She didn't like answering the phone when it rang unless it was Bernadette or me.

The company didn't like employees to be out of the office unless it was unavoidable. Clarissa was still in her trial period, and she had already called in sick a few times because her children were sick or had a doctor's appointment. When this happened, she always stayed late to make up her time. Jack wanted her replaced, and I argued that she was a hard worker and the only one who seemed to enjoy scrubbing data. I didn't want to waste time trying to find the right fit. So, she stayed.

Later with COVID, most were allowed to work from home. This was perfect for Clarissa. When she had to stay home, she worked late into the night. Her work was always on time. When she had a child, it was sadly stillborn, and had to stay home to recover. She worked almost every day, something I would have done. I tried convincing her to stay off the computer, but I understood.

An Opportunity

"Start by doing what's necessary; then what's possible; and suddenly you are doing the impossible."
—St. Francis of Assisi

I had an opportunity that I had wished for 33 years ago. The Customer Service Manager left abruptly. I remember when Jack called to tell us that she was gone, his voice was different. He sounded very sad and hurt.

I sat for about 30 minutes while the news spread throughout the office. I was thinking of a solution and ignored the talk. I picked up the phone and called Jack.

"I can help you. I can cover until you can hire someone." He didn't give me a yes or a no. I think he was stunned that I would even offer or that I had the capability to do the job.

Then Leona, the Supply Chain Manager who was also over Customer Services, takes me into an office and shuts the door. She wants to know if I was serious and convinces me that I could do the job. Then she tells me Jack was speaking to my manager. It was all going so fast. My manager calls me into his office as I walk back to my desk.

"I don't know what you said, and what you just got yourself into!" He counseled and encouraged me as he always did. He told me it was my decision, and he was okay with whatever I decided. They gave me no more than a few hours to think about it and because deep inside I knew it was what I always wanted, I accepted it.

Everything happened so fast. I was signing the job offer and to my surprise there was more money with it. The first thing I asked was "Did he do this on his own?" and Leona said "yes." Even my manager was surprised when it came across his desk for his signature. What was more surprising was that he had also given a raise to three Customer Service Reps and just a week before I was almost in tears when I heard how little they were paid, and I had made it known.

The next day, we were moved to the Customer Service area. I took my two employees and inherited another three. The first few weeks were traumatizing, and I started feeling I had made a huge mistake. I had tea in the morning and nothing until I got home after 8 at night, eating just a snack of cheese and crackers. Went to bed by 9:30 and awoke to the same routine. I did this for three weeks. Eventually my Accounts Receivable friends began to check on me. Julie would offer to bring me lunch and on occasion, I accepted, but barely touched it. We started interviewing for a Logistics position that would alleviate a lot of the stress. He couldn't come fast enough for me. This made seven employees.

Within two hours of my first day as the Customer Service Manager, I was yelled at by a sales Manager. He was furious that a shipment was missed that needed to be at a hospital the next morning. I was taken aback because it was my very first two hours on the job when I am given his call, and he begins to tell me how bad we will look when the hospital finds out that the shipment was missed. This was inconsiderate and uncalled for. What could I say, other than that I would ensure it did not happen again. I didn't even know what was missed, nor where it was going, or which Customer Service Rep caused the shipment error. I couldn't do anything about it this day but knew that the next days were going to be challenging and I was ready for them. At least I thought so.

This new set-up was more than I could handle. I did all I could to not show my emotions and fears. The International shipments and dealing with the different Country personalities was also an eye opener. There was one person who sent BOLD UPPER CAPS and highlighted in yellow emails. He was very upset that we could not create his documents as his country required them for shipment. We couldn't find examples of what was previously prepared, and so Donald and the IT group helped me, and this man was still not happy with anything. He finally found some examples I could use to properly ship his orders.

Donald had to calm me down a few times when I became emotional and tired and felt at my lowest. He told me that what I did in volunteering for the temporary management position was admirable. That made me a little nervous, because I thought he was going to say something negative, but it was all good! I was falling apart, and he picked me up.

At this point, I wasn't sure who my manager was. Leona managed the Customer Center. She helped me manage the employees and then she was busy with the production side and was involved in so many other aspects of the company. I still leaned on Donald. Then I had Jack who gave me orders and began to feel that I was working more for him than the other two.

One day after a couple of months into the position, I peeked into Donald's office to ask him if he missed me and, in the conversation, he told me that in his entire career, he had never known someone like me, with my work ethic and the challenges I took on. This is a highly respected man who has very high expectations of his employees, so when he was giving me these compliments, I quietly listened and for the first time in my life I believed in my self-worth. This is a conversation that will stay with me forever.

We also had to have invoices prepared before a container could be shipped. The big truck with the loaded container was charging us a fee for wait time. One night, I was still typing invoices and I couldn't see the screen anymore. Jack and Sedra, the senior Customer Service Rep, were waiting for me so that we could all walk out together. Sedra suggested I increase the screen size. Duh! I didn't think of that. Sedra was very knowledgeable in almost all aspects of the Customer Service Center, so I leaned on her when I had questions or doubts. I couldn't think anymore. Jack saw how I was struggling with my vision, so he sat down and typed it for me while I read off the numbers. That was surprising and more so for Sedra. We finally convinced Jack to rehire a very knowledgeable employee who was an expert in international shipments. She was a blessing to all of us. I was now managing eight employees.

After about seven months of trying to keep on top of all the shipment issues and customer issues and keeping up with my Rebates and Data Entry employees, I was having panic attacks. I finally spoke with Jack one day when he was in town. I explained that I was having an attack on my way to the distribution center.

"Has this ever happened before?" he asked.

"No, because I've never had so many critical responsibilities and we need to hire someone soon or I won't make it for another month." I said this all-in-one breath!

We did eventually hire someone who was very qualified. And I went back to my original responsibilities.

It felt like the tension was over. I was more relaxed and so were the Customer Service Reps. Customer Service became the snack place. Someone was bringing something to share with the group. We had donuts, Mexican sweets, candy, and what not. Jack loved the cochitos, so every so often he'd pull out a 20-dollar bill and hand it to one of the Customer Service Reps to buy him a box of cochitos. During the holidays, I brought in baklava and a special box for Jack thinking he'd take it home, but it was gone before the day was over.

I became ill with COVID, with terrible headaches, and a lot of congestion, but fortunately didn't get other symptoms like a fever and body aches. The headaches were the worst. I had to hold my head up even watching TV. The booster shots weren't out yet and so having a low immune system from Rheumatoid

Arthritis and being diabetic, the illness lingered on. Jack and Mack called to check on me regularly. Jack arranged to have one of his customers bring an oximeter to my home. My oxygen was normal so that took one worry away.

During the holidays, my father-in-law passed away from age issues and 18 days later COVID took my mother-in-law. It was a sad time for the family.

It seemed that the whole office environment changed during and after COVID. More people were working from home. Some left the company. Even management was changing, and rumors began. The company was sold and from experience, I knew what was to come, so I prepared for retirement.

The CFO and CEO of the new company were eager to meet me. When both came into my office, they asked how I knew so much. They were concerned for me. When they found out that I had also temporarily held the Customer Center Management position they asked, "How did they even allow it?"

They proceeded to tell me that at the new company there is a person who handles each of my responsibilities. One person for Special Pricing, one for Customer Number maintenance, one for Rebates, one for Admin Fees, and the list goes on! I knew I had a lot on my plate but never had the time to step back and think about it. I just moved along day after day doing what needed to be done.

I learned that mental work was more stressful than physical work. With physical stress, you could go home and sit with a glass of wine and the body calms down. With mental stress, the mind keeps working, looking for answers, preparing for the next day.

This reminds me of the many times, I got sleepy while driving after a long day or a long week of work. It was a Saturday and I had gone to get my hair done. My hairdresser is Karla, my cousin's ex-wife who I have followed no matter what location in town she works at. This time it was on the opposite side of town. On the way back, I felt my body relaxing but luckily, I had just gotten off the freeway and was driving on a quiet road. I was following a Jeep; the driver was wearing a cowboy hat. I was thinking it looked like a friend and the next thing, I'm waking up on the shoulder. I had fallen asleep just like that! I was so upset and shaking and thankful that my angel was watching over me. I could have gone to the left and into oncoming traffic. I also know how to ruin trips by sleeping through the beautiful scenery as I did when we were in Alaska.

The new company was trying to convince me to stay and so finally I agreed, with the condition I would work as a consultant, part-time. I was assigned to a very nice, easy-going, Sales Operations Manager. I enjoyed my time working for him. Before I left, I asked that my two remaining employees, Bernadette, and Clarissa, be left intact, and they were.

During this time, the new CFO noticed all the painted pots around the office that I had gifted to some of those that I worked with. She asked how much I charged and that she would pay me for one. I painted one for her and mailed it to her Chicago home. I didn't ask for payment but one day I received a gift card. On my final day, she sent a nice email. It was such a good way to end my career.

I wasn't done with Jack and Mack yet, though. I contracted with them to help them out on another project. It was good to still be in contact as I miss the socialization and the humor especially when Jack rattles off with one of his made-up stories that I believe until he or Mack give me the clue that it's not true.

After so many years, one night before I left the company for good, I sat at my desk looking at all the paperwork, then at my computer. I didn't have people contact like I did before. Everything was so materialistic. I felt gross not being in touch with my creativity and spirituality. At least while I was training someone or doing some project for the managers and reps, I felt like I was giving of myself and not just a robot.

Thinking Back

"Yesterday is gone. Tomorrow has not yet come.
We have only today. Let us begin."
—Mother Teresa

I have no regrets in what I experienced throughout the years. It has made it an interesting life and I wish I could experience some of it at least once more. I can truly say I was blessed with the opportunities that came my way. I am also glad that my career ended on my terms. I am forever grateful for the dean and his assistant from Pima College who started it all for me.

There were ups and downs, but the downs made me stronger. I had many managers, each with their own personalities. I know that sometimes I was not easy. I know I was hardheaded, passionate, curious, stubborn, intimidating, rough, and even a squeaky wheel! They must have all seen something good in me to have called me back so many times and even kept me when I thought I was not good enough.

I know that I gave too much of myself for so many years not just because I loved my tasks but because I challenged myself to be better than the person I used to be. I thrived doing work for those who appreciated me, and many did. There were very few who took advantage of me. In fact, it is sad to say that at a time or two my very own peers were the ones who did. I miss many of my co-workers, some who have passed away and some that I lost track of over the years. I still enjoy speaking and seeing those I stay in touch with.

It may have taken me 40 years of work and no play, but at the end when my mind and body said "enough," I became hungry for the art, crafts, and writing that I left dormant for so many years. If I had not gone through the "work" journey I would not have met the people who encouraged me and would not have the means to afford my creative addictions.

I can play with clay until it becomes the shape of a surprise, not something I was asked to make. I can cut fabric and turn it into a quilt that someone will use and remember who made it with so much love. I can paint pots all day, enjoying the many colors of paint that end up on the pots as pretty flowers or some unique design, then gifting them to family and friends.

I can read a book when I want, even though I'll forget tomorrow what it was about. I can write what I want and when I want. No one will yell at me for a mistake not mine and no one will care what color I am, nor tell me how to eat at a fancy restaurant. I can play in the sand, let my skin get dark, jump in my tub, where there is no dirty water, only sand.

I can dance when I want, and I can listen to by-gone music that is new only to me.

I can buy flowers whenever I want, enjoy them, even if they will wilt and die. I'll keep one or two to dry and continue looking at them in a vase or a pretty, empty wine bottle.

I can learn to care for Mom, even though I'll argue that I was not meant to care for others, so patience is a virtue, I will struggle to learn.

As for my parents, they always tried. They learned with their children, and we learned from their sternness and mistakes and the guilt they put us through when reprimanding us. In their quiet ways, they instilled in us hard work and less play. Everyone in our family became what my parents prayed for. We were all successful even through struggles, insecurities, and fears, but we had guidance, love, and most of all prayer, faith, and hope.

The black sheep turned attractive enough for the women who told me I was pretty, boys who flirted with me, men who dated me and finally the man I married.

In my adult years when I felt the roller coaster moving faster, I slowed it down in the quiet of the night. I thought about my past and I found myself longing for the simple summers in Rayón, taking my siesta under the bed. Thinking of the hand-me-downs, the old Barbies, the old bicycles, the adolescent body, the old car, and the hard-earned Popsicles but most of all I craved being in a house with all my siblings, planning a new play, while Mom sits under a lamp, knitting yet another baby sweater, and Dad sits in "his" chair with his fifth cup of coffee in one hand and his cigarette in the other.

What I am today is because of yesterday. I don't regret having little as a child, nor the absence of a degree. Instead, I learned to work hard for what I am and what I own today. I learned to be compassionate with those who have less. I learned to love even those who hurt me. I also learned to do everything with passion. If passion is absent, so am I.

We continue to visit Colorado to visit Melissa and to enjoy the scenery.

…but Tucson is where my heart is content.

LEGEND – *Description of titles and responsibilities during the years of my employment. Descriptions are not in detail. The corporation descriptions may be different from the medical company, at the end of my career, as noted.*

- *Accounts Receivable (A/R) – Collect payments from customers and works closely with the CSR and sales reps to resolve issues. Also work with sales on special agreed to contracts that may include purchase discounts and/or credits.*

- *Branch Managers – Manage a sales branch that includes the Sales Managers and their group of Sales Reps.*

- *Business Analyst – At the corporation, it is the person who supports the Sales Managers and their regions. They are a liaison between the CSR, the Rep, and the Manager. They also resided in the Region they were assigned to (in the 1990's).*

- *Business Partner (BP) – A company who is contracted with a manufacturing company to sell their products to the end-user customer. They order in bulk and keep product on hand at their warehouse or distribution centers. The BP is compensated via a Rebate or other agreed to plan for the sales. Payment is made only after the BP submits detailed sales reports back to the company they have the contract with.*

- *Chief Executive Officer (CEO) – Head of the company and accountable for business decisions and business success.*

- *Chief Financial Officer (CFO) – Handles the budget and works with the Accountants, Sales Management, Production, Administration, and many other departments.*

- *Commission Analyst - This position is that of an administrator who implements the approved sales compensation plan then generates the final monthly sales reports that are used for calculating commissions. Works closely with the sales team, finance and all Operations Managers and Business Analysts.*

In my case, I also handled the territory program and managed the product categories and globally wrote the quota guidelines based on Finance and Sales Operations input. (Other companies may include their unique list of responsibilities.)

- *Customer Support Rep (CSR) – Medical company refers to this position as "Customer Service Rep" and most recently as "Customer Care Rep"*

  o *Administrator who supports the Sales Reps*
  o *Assists customers with their orders, contracts, product shipments and billing.*
  o *Works with Accounts Receivable*
  o *Enriched CSR – Enriched Customer Support Rep*
    - *Same duties as the CSR but included invoicing the customer and following up with payment.*

- *Customer Service Rep (the corporation – in the '80s and and '90s) – Services the product sold.*

- *Maintenance Rep – Sold maintenance after warranty expires.*

- *Marketing Administrative Assistant – Assisted Sales Reps with sales and contracts and was the liaison between the CSR and the Reps and works directly with the customer.*

- *Region Manager – Same as a Sales Manager but covered a whole Region.*

- *Sales Director – Managed all Region Managers*

- *Sales Manager – Manages a group of Sales Reps within a Region*

- *Sales Operations Manager – The Sales Operations Manager in Atlanta Headquarters handled all aspects of the sales administration organization and worked closely with the CFO and CEO and the sales management. This position also worked with the Divisions and Branches and with the U.S. Commission Analyst (me).*

- *Note: This position was also assigned to an individual in each country and like the Business Analyst role in the U.S. with additional responsibilities. They later became my commission contacts.*

- *Sales Representative (Sales Rep) – Sellers of company's hardware products, software, and services.*

- *Software & Service Engineer – Sells software for hardware products and works with customer during installation of product and supports the sales rep if needed to close a sale.*

  o *System Engineer (title used in later years) – same as the Software & Service Engineer except "Service" became its own department selling services.*

- *Technical Service Rep – Repairs the product and includes selling parts.*

Acknowledgements

First and foremost, I thank my brothers and sisters, who encouraged me to finish my story and who were patient with me when I needed advice. I thank my siblings' spouses and my in-laws for their curiosity and support. I also thank my 92-year-old mom who laughs when I remind her of her cruel comments and then apologizes. She also gave me invaluable stories of her life. I thank my tías Josefina Rodriguez and Amelia Tasler Carlin who brought back memories of my time in Rayón. I thank Ana Capogrosso, my cousin, who gave me current information, as one of the youngest cousins who experienced the modernized town of Rayón.

I thank Tom Bird, Tom Bird Seminars, Inc. for convincing me to finish my memoir and for his gentle coaching and guidance through the end.

I thank Elena Diaz Bjorkquist who inspired me through her books and for encouraging me to write when I had thoughts that I was not good enough. I thank Geneva Maria Escobedo, Flora Gamez Grateron, and Mari Herreras for inspiring me with their most recent published books.

295

I thank Rita Gonzales Boepple whom I barely knew, who was so kind as to take my memoir draft home to read and return it all marked with great suggestions. I was heartbroken to hear she had passed soon after when I recently contacted her dear friend, Nina, asking for Rita's email. Thank you, Nina, for sharing her story.

Finally, I thank my husband, Ralph, who I constantly interrupted with questions when I was stuck on a word or phrase. I thank him for helping with dinner when he plainly saw I was not budging from my desk. Most of all, I thank him for always supporting and encouraging me to write (and paint). I thank our daughter, Melissa, for correcting me when an event was different from her view and for believing in my writing journey.

Finally, I thank God, my Creator, who gave me the courage to pursue my dreams. He, who guided me throughout my work, and where edits were made through his persistence and my obedience.

www.ingramcontent.com/pod-product-compliance
Lightning Source LLC
Chambersburg PA
CBHW051942090426
42741CB00008B/1242